PICKLEBALL
IS LIFE

PICKLEBALL
IS LIFE

THE COMPLETE GUIDE TO
FEEDING YOUR OBSESSION

ERIN McHUGH

HARVEST

An Imprint of WILLIAM MORROW

HarperCollins books may be purchased for educational, business, or sales promotional use. For information, please email the Special Markets Department at SPsales@harpercollins.com.

FIRST EDITION

Designed by Tai Blanche

Illustrations by Jackie Besteman

Artwork of net on page 118–119 © Jollanda/Shutterstock

Library of Congress Cataloging-in-Publication Data has been applied for.

ISBN 978-0-06-327215-6

22 23 24 25 26   WOR   10 9 8 7 6 5 4 3 2 1

To all the kind and glorious people who have included me, taught me, coached me, and made me laugh, learn, and feel welcome on my ever-expanding pickleball journey. You know who you are. You sure make life fun.

Contents

Introduction |||||||||||||||||||||||||||||||||||| 1

Tales from the Kids of
Summer 3

Not Your Grandpa's
Shuffleboard 14

Getting Started |||||||||||||||||||||||||||||||| 16

Paddles 18

Balls 23

Demo Paddle Programs 27

A Quick Warm-Up 28

The Serve 29

Scoring 35

DIY Pickleball Court 40

The Quirky Rules 49

The Lingo 60

Para Pickleball 66

The Names of the Games 67

Road Tennis: Pickleball's
Distant Cousin 71

Glow-in-the-Dark
Pickleball 72

Off-Season Training Tips 75

The Pickleverse ||||||||||||||||||||||||| 76

The Players 78

Accessories 86

The Après-Pickle Life 93

10 Important Things I'd Rather Do Than Play Pickleball 100

Pickleball Is Life: The Greats Speak Out 101

The Cancel-O-Meter 107

Lies to Tell to Get Out of Something and Play Pickleball Instead 109

My Changing World 112

The Pickleball Hall of Fame 114

Celebrities: Obsessed Like Us 115

Etiquette |||||||||||||||||||||||||||||||||| 118

The Do's and Don'ts 121

Salty Language 123

Complimenting the Opposition: Yea or Nay? 124

The Art of Trash-Talking 125

Play Up and Play Down 129

Target Practice 130

There's No Sorry in Pickleball 132

Living Your Best Pickleball Life ||||| 134

Bringing Pickleball to Your Community: 5 Easy Tips 137

Be a Pickleball Ambassador 138

Your Best Pickleball Life 140

My Pickleball Journey 148

||||||||||||||||||||||||||||||||||||||||||||

Acknowledgments 151

Introduction

Once upon a time, an unexpected thing happened: I broke my hand. Luckily, it wasn't too, too serious, but still. It meant I couldn't play pickleball. I was going to be on the disabled list for *ten endless weeks*, and I couldn't imagine how I would get through it.

Oh, I tried my best. I attempted a jigsaw puzzle, all the while thinking of pickleball. I took long walks, thinking of pickleball. I worked one-handed in my garden, thinking—well, you know.

I could barely recall what I'd done with my time in my pre-pickleball life. I started to ruminate about why I had come to love the sport so much. Certainly, it was the simple fun of the game, and the laughter, but it was the friendship and socializing, too. And the gamesmanship, and court etiquette, and how fit I'd become, and how it reminded me (after living in a New York City apartment for forty-two years) how much I love the outdoors. But I also realized it went deeper than all that: this nutty game was making me kinder, more inclusive, and more strategic, not to mention a much more skilled trash-talker. Pickleball is inspirational, I concluded, so why not share this epiphany with my fellow picklers, in the most lighthearted, yet motivational, way? So I sat down and wrote this book (one-handed) about the most special, most obsessive, most enjoyable game on the planet.

If you're already a pickleballer, I hope you'll enjoy a little armchair reading, have some laughs, and garner some extra knowledge about our favorite pastime. If you're a new player, I'll introduce you to the game's ineffable charm and maybe even provide you with a few secret weapons.

But, even with a broken hand and a book deadline, I couldn't help myself. I went out and learned to play pickleball with my other hand.

Because, friends, if you didn't already know, PICKLEBALL IS LIFE!

Tales FROM THE Kids OF Summer

We fanatics of the game all scour the internet, gobbling up anything and everything we can find about how our passion came to be. Pickleball started small, a local game among friends in 1965 on Bainbridge Island, Washington. In an attempt to keep their kids occupied, some dads on vacation cobbled together a game in a backyard with a salvaged net, a plastic ball, and some beat-up Ping-Pong paddles. What began as a diversion to while away an afternoon became the neighborhood obsession. Other families joined in, the adults became more and more interested, and soon playing pickleball was a daily activity.

These summer folks brought the new sport back to Seattle and its environs, where many of them lived, and occasionally one of their summer guests would even return to their own city or town with tales of this crazy game their friends had invented. In this way, pickleball became somewhat of an underground pastime, gaining popularity in Washington State and pockets around the country. It took a decade for pickleball's origin story to get picked up as a human interest piece by some national press, and then another ten years passed before it had enough of a foothold that players became interested in having better equipment, and a national association was founded.

People really began to hear about pickleball in the early 2000s, mostly from friends playing it in retirement communities

FRANK PRITCHARD

or on winter vacations in the sunshine states—or even from their kids, who often played it in gym class indoors in the winter months. But in recent years, its growth has been exponential, and the sport that people thought was for their grandparents now has a median playing age in the thirties. Everywhere you look, there are families playing, kids playing, or people searching for courts to play on, repurposing spaces wherever they can find them.

It's not often you can reach back to the beginning when you're researching history—to check with the source or ask a question you yearn to know the answer to. Lucky for us, pickleball is a relatively new game, and while the original three men who got this unique pastime started—Joel Pritchard, Bill Bell, and Barney McCallum—are no longer with us, their children are. And the memories of how these families devised a game for them all to play is still very fresh in the minds of those kids who were there that summer.

As legend has it, Frank Pritchard was a bored kid who voiced that universal childhood complaint: "There's nuthin' to *do* around here."

I was lucky enough to track Frank down, and he freely admitted to being this now-famous bored kid. Ladies and gentlemen, a standing ovation, please, to Frank Pritchard. Show him your eternal thanks. Without him, there would be no pickleball.

Frank laid down the gauntlet when I spoke to him at his home in Washington State. He laughed and said, "This is how religious wars begin. Everybody has their take on it, and they truly believe their side. But I'm going to tell you the truth.

"I probably had what I've heard referred to as 'resting bitch face,'" he said. "Or more accurately, the 'I hate this place, I hate my life, and I *really* hate your attempts to suggest things for me to do' face. You know, a typical, well-rounded thirteen-year-old boy. My wife would tell you that I've segued from whining to bitching. It's more adult."

Frank sounded to me like he was a man who would indeed tell the truth. He started by describing his family's summer getaway on Bainbridge, which was much more rustic back in the 1960s than it is now. "My grandparents had this sort of compound, and we had a goofy old house," he began. "When I complained to my father that day, his retort was, 'Well, you know, when *we* were kids here, we used to make games up.' And I said, 'Oh, really? Why don't *you* go make a game up, then.'"

Frank's grandparents were big badminton players in their day and had a court on their property, he recalled. He'd been given a Wiffle ball and bat for a recent birthday, and it had lain around, unused. His father, Joel, picked it up, walked to the back of the property, and went to work.

Allison Bell Wood, pickleball coinventor Bill Bell's daughter, was about seven years old that summer, but she clearly remembers the first day of playing. "Oh yeah! Because the big kids didn't want the little kids playing, too," she said. "You know how at the beginning of something, it's so exciting? We all loved it, but the little kids were complaining because the big kids didn't want to let us play. But I think it was Joel and my dad who helped navigate it from the beginning to figure out how everyone got a turn."

Joel Pritchard and Bill Bell were great friends, and the Bells were renting a house that summer on Bainbridge. (In fact, Frank and Allison and their families are still as close as their parents were.) And though it was the kids who instigated the game, Allison recalls, "The adults took it over pretty quickly. Cocktails were always involved from the beginning in pickleball. My guess is a lot of gin and beer."

Frank recalled that his dad and Bill started the process of getting the fun going, and Frank was kind of standing there, taking it all in. And then his dad said, "You know what we need? We need Barney." And off they went to grab pickleball founder number three.

Barney McCallum and his family lived about six doors down, and Joel and Barney had worked together. Barney was a creative, clever guy, and it wouldn't be a bad idea to pick his brain, Joel thought. Barney immediately got on board, and he remained devoted to the sport until he died in 2019 at ninety-three years old.

What about the rules? I wondered. How did this thing even get *loosely* organized?

"Some things had to be addressed right away," Allison said. "We were just hitting [the ball] back and forth, and then the parents said, 'Hey, wait, this is a lot of fun,' and they even started playing with the kids, which was a rare thing, to play with your kids in those days. But almost instantly, since Joel and Dad were huge control freaks, they started making up the rules. For example, the Brown brothers and their dad, other local friends, were so tall that suddenly my father said, 'You can't

stand at the net.' They drew a line down and said, 'You can't go any closer than this.' That's how the kitchen came to be—and I think it was Aunt Joan Pritchard who said, 'Well, if you can't stand the heat, stay out of the kitchen!'" And there you are.

Frank and Allison agreed—a lot of pickleball's rules developed much later, when it became more widespread and accepted as a sport. Frank recalled, "The original rules were that it was scored like badminton. You served crosscourt, one foot out and one foot in. You had to serve underhand. To score, you had to be serving."

But what about the net, the paddles?

"We had a building on the property, and my dad went up there and he found a badminton net. He fixed the net to his waist height. And they kind of started screwing around with it."

Allison remembered the adults stripping the rubber off some old Ping-Pong paddles. But Barney got going with constructing the equipment right away. Frank said, "We had some crude paddles, and Barney cut the first real paddle [out] of plywood, and that design kind of stayed with us for years."

Frank and I laughed—it wasn't so different in shape from what we have today, we agreed.

They all—parents and kids alike—played pickleball constantly over the next several years on the island. The original court is still there, and occasionally used, although the property is now owned by another family. But in the years right after 1965, each of the founders did his own version of serving as an ambassador of the sport.

Joel Pritchard went into politics and became a member of Congress and eventually Washington's lieutenant governor. When he was on the road making political appearances, he'd take a net and some paddles and balls along with him. The minute the crowd began to get restless, Pritchard would shout, "Let's play some pickleball!" This helped pickleball become well-known throughout the state. And possibly helped Pritchard get elected.

Businessman Bill Bell gets the credit for taking pickleball global. After leaving Seattle, he and his family moved to New York City (where, in 1967, they taped a court down indoors at the Brooklyn Heights Casino, a squash, tennis, and social club), and then overseas. The Bells lived in Australia, Singapore, Hong Kong, and Indonesia—and they took pickleball with them wherever they went. "Our backyard in Jakarta was a pickleball court!" Allison recalls. "We would have pickleball parties and tournaments there all the time with the other expats in the early 1970s."

But both Allison and Frank agreed: the lifelong pickleball ambassador was Barney McCallum. "Barney would be looked at by many to be the father of pickleball, because once the summers were over, Joel would go back to Congress in D.C., and we moved away. And then David, Barney's son, took over the growing Pickle-Ball, Inc., business Barney started in 1972," Allison said. "Back in the day we called David 'Clutch' because he had the *most* groovy car," she remembered with a laugh. "The McCallums took the game from something the families all did together to what it has become."

Frank agreed wholeheartedly. "Barney really deserves credit for nurturing pickleball, and feeding it, and bringing it along. It wouldn't be what it is today if he hadn't stuck with it. He was the guy that did the hard work."

I asked them what their families had taken away from this weird and magical ride and what they see when they look at pickleball, then and now.

Allison thought a moment before she answered. "People just thought it was a crazy game. But it was a connector. I find this whole thing with what's happened with pickleball just amazing, because it was nothing more than a fluke that it even started that day.

"What's really been impressive to me is that the passion of a whole group of people who've got nothing to do with Bainbridge or the Pacific Northwest has taken it to a completely different dynamic," she continued. "It's wonderful, and it just shows you the fun of the game. We remember our family experiences with it. That's really what it was about for us." When I told her the title of this book, Allison laughed. "Pickleball *is* life," she agreed, "and it reminds you that you can always learn to do new things and have fun. If it's one thing I've learned, it's a game that spans generations, and spans interests.

"It's just accessible. You can play the game almost instantly. You can go out and after fifteen minutes figure out the rhythm of the ball. It's always fun. It's easy to go out and play a quick game. You can't do that with tennis, or golf, or squash, but you can with pickleball."

Frank is equally dumbfounded. "My family is just amazed. I mean, it just isn't real. It isn't real!" I asked him how this unexpected legacy made him feel. "More than anything," Frank mused, "my father would be so thrilled. He was kind of like a camp counselor, and he loved getting people up moving and playing games. It just gave him a thrill. I think if he knew how many people got such pleasure out of this thing—besides exercise and mental health and physical health—I think that would be to him the greatest thing of all."

And finally, readers, to address the topic you've all been wondering about: What is the genesis of the name pickleball? How did this nutty name come to this insane game? Was it, in fact, named after a dog, as popular legend has it?

1965

A combination of boredom, friendship, and a lazy summer sparks the invention of pickleball by three families on Bainbridge Island, Washington.

1967

The first permanent pickleball court is built by cofounder Joel Pritchard's neighbor, Bob O'Brian.

1972

Pickle-Ball, Inc., is founded as a corporation to protect the creation of the sport. Barney McCallum eventually buys out his partners and passes the company to his son David. OLLA, LLC, now owns and operates the company, whose motto still has a homey ring: "We believe the best employees and partners play pickleball. Seriously."

SPOILER ALERT

Allison was adamant in her reply: "The dog came after the game. It was the boat."

And Frank ought to know; Pickles, the cockapoo, was his dog. "Pickles came to us in 1968, *three years later*. She was cute, sweet, and smart—but she never went up to the court, never chased the ball."

How did this canine myth stick, all these decades later?

The dog, obviously, *was* named after the game. "It got to be part of the story of the game's history," said Frank. "And in 1975, a guy from the *National Observer* came to the island to do what was to be the first big media feature on the game. During the interview, someone told him the story people were telling, that the game was named for our dog, Pickles—though that wasn't the truth! And he said, 'Oh, the dog story is cute. Let's stick with that.'"

That's right, friends: *fake news*. That's how the story was printed. The name of the game actually came from Joan Pritchard, Frank's mother. She said the ragtag nature of the game reminded her of the rowing term "pickle boat," which refers to a crew team that has been thrown together from random available rowers. Joan and Joel met at Marietta College, which had a popular crew team, and then they moved to Seattle, where the University of Washington always has had a renowned rowing program. So, though the term "pickle boat" may not enjoy wide usage, it was part of the Pritchards' vocabulary—and a funny, fitting name for this scrubby backyard game.

A DOG NAMED Pickles

COCKAPOO

"I think the pickle boat is so indicative of the game—an amalgamation of a lot of things and racket sports put together to create this quirky game," said Frank. And then he paused. "My mother never got credit for naming this thing. It's been one of my little missions in life to get this story straight."

So, here's to you, Joan Pritchard! The record is being set straight at last. Thanks for coming up with the most stellar name for the world's most obsessive game.

Not YOUR Grandpa's Shuffleboard

What is this thing called pickleball? The court's a little like this, the scoring's a little like that, the paddle's reminiscent of something else. People say it's a mash-up of badminton, tennis, and Ping-Pong, and certainly the three founders had some of each in mind when they started playing and slowly set up some rules. But how, exactly, have these sports left their mark on pickleball?

PING-PONG—There are lots of details about the pickleball paddle that will remind you of a Ping-Pong paddle. It's short and has no strings—not at all like a tennis racket. Some of the first paddles the families on Bainbridge Island used were old Ping-Pong paddles with the rubber stripped off. And Ping-Pong is the only one of these three sports that has a winning game score of 11, which you must win by two points—just like pickleball.

TENNIS—Like tennis, pickleball is played on a court. However, the pickleball court is about one-quarter the size of a tennis court—and there are no alleys: doubles and singles games are both played in the same area. In tennis you serve overhand and get two chances to land your serve in the box. Not so in pickleball: the serve is underhand with only one chance to get it right. Lots of racket people play both games.

BADMINTON—The dimensions of a badminton court are exactly the same as that of a pickleball court. This similarity is not just a coincidence: the original court used for pickleball on Bainbridge Island was an old badminton court.

No matter what the racket or paddle sport is, though, they all have one irksome goal in common: you still have to get the damn thing—whether it's a ball or a shuttlecock—over the net.

1975

The first big-time article about pickleball appears in the *National Observer*. The reporter later calls Barney McCallum and asks if he'd be interested in selling kits of pickleball equipment. Pickle-Ball, Inc., begins packaging a box with a net, 4 paddles, 12 balls, and some instructions for $29.50. Orders immediately stream in.

1976

Tennis magazine publishes an article, "America's Newest Racquet Sport." But for the cognoscenti, the secret has already been out.

1976

Competition gets real: the first known pickleball tournament is held, at the South Center Athletic Club in Tukwila, Washington.

Getting

Started

Paddles

It's not unusual to feel like you don't even know where to start when you're looking for a pickleball paddle. Maybe it's your first, or maybe you're looking to upgrade; either way, you'll have lots of questions. And the truth is, it's not so easy to walk into a sporting goods store or pro shop and find a wall full of paddles to pick up and inspect.

The search itself can be confusing. Once you go down the paddle search rabbit hole, you'll find that the surfaces can be one of four different kinds of material: graphite, composite, carbon fiber, or wood. And those are just the faces! Once you've digested *that* for a bit, you'll discover there are three kinds of interior cores: polypropylene (or polycore), Nomex, and aluminum. You can do a deep dive into the options, and maybe

The Original   Today

even enjoy all that research, but in the meantime, here is a short summary of helpful paddle facts.

Paddles are usually referred to by the material on their faces. **Graphite** paddles are the most widely used. They tend to be quite light, and you'll likely find you have more control with them than with other types of paddles. That said, a **composite** paddle will give your shots extra power. They are usually a bit heavier than other paddles. So, think about your game: what you're good at, and what you'd like to improve on. If it's finesse you're looking for, choose graphite. If you want some bang— maybe your drive isn't as monstrous as you'd like—look at the composite options. **Carbon fiber** paddles are among the most expensive, and the lightest. You'll probably get the best ball control from them, but you'll lose that power touch, since carbon fiber is the softest of the three options discussed so far. And then there's the old standby, the original **wood** paddle. First of all, these are very heavy, and they don't offer much control. If you're looking to buy a passel of paddles for your local high school or YMCA, though, these could be the ticket because they are the least expensive options. (Speaking of costs: If you'd just

Regulation Paddle Size

As per the USAPA (USA Pickleball Association or USA Pickleball, the governing body for the sport) specs, there is a limit set for a paddle's size. To be considered legal, the length plus the width must not exceed 24 inches; the length alone cannot exceed 17 inches. So be mindful that if you choose an elongated paddle, you'll lose some width.

like to try your hand at pickleball and aren't ready to shell out for expensive equipment, you can purchase a bundle, which often includes four paddles and four balls; shell out a little more and they'll throw in a portable net, too. But if you're purchasing only for yourself, and you think you might really be interested in pickleball—and why wouldn't you be?—a small investment will get you a perfectly good paddle to start your adventure.)

Most paddles have a honeycomb structure inside, and this core hasn't changed much since the mid-1980s. A material known as **Nomex** was used back then and is still a great choice today. Newer technology has introduced **polymer**, or **polypropylene**, cores to the market. Because paddles with this type of interior are the quietest, you may want to choose them if you live in a community or neighborhood where there may be noise complaints—or even noise restrictions. They are also the

Paddles by Weight

LIGHTWEIGHT 7.2 ounces and under

MIDDLEWEIGHT 7.3 to 8.3 ounces

HEAVYWEIGHT 8.3 ounces and over

Grip Circumferences

SMALL 4 inches

MEDIUM 4⅛ inches to 4¼ inches

LARGE 4½ inches

softest paddles—so expect less power when playing with them—but you may find you get a bit more control as a trade-off. **Aluminum** cores are the lightest of all, and are a great option if you've got arthritis or a shoulder or elbow problem, or if you're outfitting a youngster, for example. But remember: you will sacrifice lots of power by playing with such a light instrument.

There are two more recent developments in paddle construction you might like to keep your eye on: the edgeless paddle and the elongated paddle. The **edgeless** version has an obvious plus: lots of those mishits into the ether from the ball catching on the rim of your present paddle will disappear like magic! The downside is that without that protective rim, the paddle face will chip more easily with use. The **elongated** paddle is a favorite of many high-level players for two reasons: it gives you just that much more reach, and the size makes the sweet spot a little bit larger.

Still baffled? If you're able to test out a few different paddles, you can

1976

Seattle's new state-of-the-art stadium, the Kingdome, opens and becomes home to many Seattle-based sports teams. But the first sport to be played at the Kingdome? Pickleball.

1978

Pickleball is first mentioned as a sport of note in a book, *The Other Racquet Sports*, by Dick Squires. The author helped to popularize the sport of platform tennis and is known throughout the sporting world as "Mr. Paddle."

1984

The United States Amateur Pickleball Association is founded to perpetuate the growth and advancement of the sport nationwide. The first official rulebook is published this year.

1984

Arlen Paranto and his son, Steve, become pickleball fanatics—and everything changes in the pickleball equipment world. An industrial engineer at Boeing, Arlen designs a lightweight composite paddle from some leftover honeycomb panels used for airplane floors. This paddle is much lighter and more responsive than the era's wooden paddles. Suddenly everyone wants one, so Paranto starts Pro-Lite Sports and begins manufacturing the paddles himself.

1999

The first pickleball website, Pickleball Stuff, appears, both selling equipment and offering information on the burgeoning sport.

begin to find what weight seems comfortable to you, and what size grip fits the best. Those two factors should be high priorities in your decision-making. Many experts say the deciding factor is always going to be that ineffable something that makes a paddle feel just right in your hand, in that Goldilocks kind of way that you can't describe.

Your best bet is to shake hands with as many paddles as you can, write down the specs of each one, and then begin your real search. Most retailers will let you return an item within a specified amount of time, so take that into consideration. Also, ask your friends. Maybe try someone's paddle for a game or two. You can find more information on procuring **demo paddles** in the section "Demo Paddle Programs" on page 27.

The bottom line to picking your paddle?

It's personal.

Balls

An essential part of pickleball lore—confirmed by Frank Pritchard—tells us that the first ball used back on that summer day in 1965 was a Wiffle ball from a bat and ball set that was lying around. From that start came the basis of what we play with today.

Here's the most important fact about the pickleball, and you'd be surprised at how many players—even the most avid—aren't aware of this: there are indoor balls, and there are outdoor balls. It's easy to tell them apart: the indoor ball has 26 holes, and the

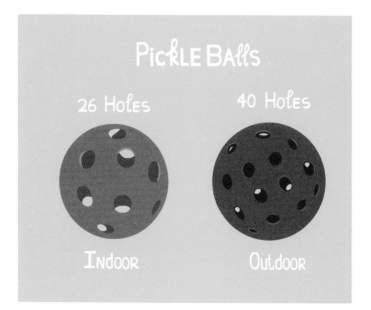

outdoor ball has 40. If you've never noticed, put the balls side by side, and the difference is immediately apparent. You may wonder if it matters which ball you use, and the answer is yes. Here's why.

The indoor ball is lighter and softer than the outdoor ball. The bounce won't be as pronounced as that of an outdoor ball, but it's perfect for a climate-controlled court.

The outdoor ball is harder, has got more bounce to it, and is heavier. When the wind picks up, you want some heft to your ball.

How long will a pickleball last? A ball may simply get a soft spot or lose some bounce after a while. And, naturally, it'll depend on what kind of game you're playing: a dinking game is easier on a ball, and a slam-bang match may split it right in half. Cold outdoor temperatures take their toll on a pickleball in a big way. If you're playing in near- or below-freezing weather, and you're smacking the ball around pretty hard, you may lose a few balls to cracking or splitting in just a single match.

For both indoor and outdoor play, try a variety of ball brands. You'll find ones you like, and new varieties appear on the market all the time. The USA Pickleball Association has applied standards and specifications for balls used in tournaments and now even the regular Joe Pickle listens up for what to choose, even for social play.

Perhaps you're wondering why pickleballs come in so many different colors. They tend to be bright for visibility. Yellow and green are the most commonly used colors, but you may prefer neon orange or pink. Depending on your outdoor surroundings, any of these bright colors can really help you track the ball during play. They stand out when there's a snowy or sandy background. On the other hand, if you're surrounded by autumn foliage, you may prefer to stick with pink.

"But it doesn't bounce!"

So very true. And guess what? A pickleball is not supposed to bounce much. When the sport was invented, rules started to formulate—like the addition of the kitchen, to help keep the big, scary players at arm's length. A ball that won't injure a player was also part of the original scheme, so Wiffle balls, and then the equally soft Cosom Fun Ball, were used for years.

2005

Mark Friedenberg establishes the USA Pickleball Association (USAPA), which has the same mission as its predecessor, the United States Amateur Pickleball Association: to promote the development and growth of the sport in the United States.

2008

The USAPA publishes the first handbook for rules of tournament play.

More recently, since the USAPA has begun to regulate how pickleballs are made, part of testing them is checking the bounce. For tournament play, when dropped from a height of 78 inches, a new ball should bounce 30 to 34 inches—and no higher.

Demo Paddle Programs

If you search the websites of different paddle manufacturers, you'll find some that will send you several paddles to try out for a week or two, often for just the cost of a shipping fee. But also, as of this writing, some pickleball equipment sites will do one better: they'll offer paddle loans from various manufacturers—and you can get several at a time.

Here are a few places to start looking online:

Total Pickleball (totalpickleball.com) will let you choose three paddles to test for seven days; all you have to pay is the shipping cost.

With Pickleball Galaxy's program (pickleballgalaxy.com), you can try two paddles for seven days, for a fee that includes shipping and a credit if you end up buying one of the paddles. The big plus is the large array of different paddles they offer for demo purposes.

You can try out a paddle from places like Pickleball Central (pickleballcentral.com) and other online retailers that allow you to return an item within thirty days.

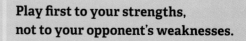

PRO TIP Play first to your strengths, not to your opponent's weaknesses.

A Quick Warm-Up

It's not a good idea to head for the pickleball court with your body all tight and then put it through its paces—especially first thing in the morning when you haven't yet revved up your chassis for the day. Try these easy exercises and stretches; not only will they get your body loosened up and help prevent injury, but they could actually help improve your game. Five to ten minutes of warm-up before you play can make all the difference.

A QUICK JOG: Once around the court or even in your yard before you get in the car to go to the court will get your heart pumping.

SIDE SHUFFLES: Starting with your feet wide apart, move laterally across the back tape of the court. Then get fancy, and cross one foot over the other as you shuffle.

HIP AND ANKLE ROTATIONS: For the hip, lift your knee waist-high and swivel in a circle several times, then reverse the direction. For the ankle, lift your foot and rotate it in a circle several times, again in both directions. Repeat each exercise

---

Don't Cross the Line

An easy mistake to make after you return a deep serve is to unwittingly step a foot or so inside the baseline. It's an anticipatory reflex but can get you in big trouble if the ball comes back to the tape again. Right behind the lines—kitchen or baseline—is where you want to be.

on the other leg. If your balance is iffy, hold on to the net post or fence.

TORSO TWIST: With your hands on your waist, move your shoulders 90 degrees one way, back to the center, and then to the other side.

ARM SWINGS: With your legs shoulder-width apart, stretch your arms out horizontally. Cross them in front of you and pull all the way back quickly. Do right over left, then left over right to get your shoulders and spine moving.

FORWARD FOLD: Stand with your feet shoulder-width apart and bend forward from the waist. If you can touch the ground, great—if not, go as far as is comfortable. This is a good stretch for the lower back and you'll be happy you did it when you have to lunge for that low shot.

Repeat all of the above a few times before hitting the court.

THE Serve

Picklers, we need to talk about the serve.

A pickleball serve is always underhand, and there are a couple of things you can be nabbed on, should your opponents be so inspired to call you out.

The rules can seem persnickety and complicated. Here are some salient points to remember.

- Your paddle must be moving in a forward motion during the serve.

LEGAL
SERVE

- Your entire paddle—from the very top to the end of the grip—must be located below your waist when your paddle makes contact with the ball.

- Every inch of your paddle must also be held below your wrist when you serve. If you break your wrist—that is, cock your hand upwards—to serve and the paddle head is above the top of your wrist, *that's illegal*.

- Since contact between the paddle and the ball must be made below the waist, if you serve from your side with your arm positioned straight out, *that's illegal*.

- If you flip your paddle up to deliver a nice high lob of a serve, and your grip is below your waist, but the paddle head ends up above your wrist before you hit the ball, *that's illegal*.

- If even your big toe touches the back tape as you're serving, it's a foot fault, and *that's illegal*.

This last rule comes up now and again and will cause a ruckus. The court lines, both the back line and the sidelines, have imaginary extensions. A server must make contact with the ball within the confines of the serving area. That is, you may not cross the imaginary center line of the court and serve from behind your partner's box. Additionally—and oh, this is the rule people love to fight about!—you may not serve from outside the imaginary extension of the sideline. Sure, you could get a good

PRO TIP Watch your back—never assume the point is over.

crosscourt delivery. But you know what both of these serves are? *They're illegal.*

It's understandable that when you're simply enjoying casual play, your serve may get a little slipshod, especially when you're trying out new ways to thwart your opponent. But train yourself to follow the serving rules strictly, because someone, someday, is going to catch you on your illegal serve, and you'll have to retrain yourself. Or if you try your illegal serve in a tournament? You'll be sunk.

The current official rules can be found online at USAPickleball.org and are worth a read-through if you have questions about the game.

Don't Touch the Net

When can you touch the net during play? Never.

Let's say, for example, your shirt touches the net during a point? No.

Okay, well, what if the ball dribbles over to your side and you *have* to touch the net just to reach the ball and scoop it back over? No again.

This also goes for the net posts, while we're at it. Don't touch them, either. Look closely: you'll see the posts are placed outside the confines of the court. Here's the thing: just stay away from the net.

The Drop Serve

Some players prefer to serve the ball after first letting it bounce on the court, and this kind of serve is perfectly legal. But the definition of the word "bounce" in this situation is important. A server may *drop* the ball from any natural height (so, bonus for you, tall people), and strike it as it comes up. But you may not *bounce* the ball with your hand—only drop it. Bouncing is *illegal.*

Some of the usual underhand serving rules do not apply to the drop serve, which may seem odd at first. For example, in a drop serve, contact with the ball may occur above the waist, your paddle head may be located above your wrist, and you may make contact with the ball when your paddle is held above the waist. Though these exceptions may make the drop serve sound like a serving free-for-all, think it through. Utilizing any of these options in a drop serve is almost moot—remember, the ball must be *dropped* to serve, not *bounced*. This means that neither getting your paddle into a position above your wrist nor making ball contact higher than your waist is an easy feat. The drop serve is a boon to folks with shoulder problems or serving problems, for example, but it may not allow for use of the variety of serving tricks you have in your usual serving quiver.

PRO TIP | **Master the dink—finesse is a key to victory.**

Scoring

There are several important elements of pickleball's scoring system, besides calling out the score. (We'll get to that, don't you worry.) Briefly, the following are some integral details to know.

- You can only score a point if you or your team is serving.

- The first server on a team serves until their team loses a point. Then the second server on the same team takes over, until their team again loses a point. Service then moves to the opposing team. Exception: At the beginning of a doubles game, only one player from the starting team serves (see the "Fair Game" sidebar) before the service switches to the other team after a point is lost.

- Players on the receiving side never alternate sides; only the serving side does. When the serving team wins a point and continues to serve, the serving player moves to the other serving box.

- When a team or single player starts their service, the server always begins from the right-hand side serving box.

- The game is played until one team or player reaches 11 points. Tournament play may extend that number to 15 or 21 points. In all cases, however, players must win by 2 points.

Fair Game

Why the single-server exception at the beginning of a doubles game? Since the team serving first will have an advantage, this rule prevents them from getting too much of a leg up at the start of the game. One fault, and the ball goes to the other team to serve.

- The score must be announced before each new serve by a player on the serving team, and it must be loud enough so that all players can hear it plainly.

- The correct way to call out the score at the beginning of a game is "0–0–2," as per the USAPA's official rules. The popular expression "0–0-Start" is no longer in the pickleball lexicon. To understand what these three numbers refer to, continue to the next section for more detail.

In singles scoring, there are only two numbers to call, one for each server/player. The first number is the score of the serving player: for example, 5–3 would be five points for the server and three for the opponent. In doubles scoring you add a third number to indicate the first or second server, so either 5-3-1 (the first server) or 5-3-2 (the second server). As always, you can score only when you're serving. When the server's score is an even number, the service starts from the right (or even) side of the court; when the score is odd, from the left side.

How to Call the Score

Ai-yi-yi.

Oy vey.

#@&*!

You're not alone if you think the hardest part of pickleball is keeping score. Having to keep track of those three numbers before every serve may seem too taxing for lots of people. Some say it's meant to be a memory trick to keep your brain agile. But really, how hard could it be? You used to have to remember your phone number, and that was seven digits. Scoring is an essential part of the game, and, technically, you're obligated to not only know what it is, but also say it aloud when it's your turn to serve.

The three numbers are:

First number—the score of the serving team (you).

Second number—the score of the receiving team (them).

Third number—who on your team is serving, the first or second server. This number is always 1 or 2.

So, for example, you would call out 7–4–2 if your team (the serving team) has 7 points, the receiving team has 4 points, and you are the second server on the serving team (again, your team).

Rally Scoring: Short and Sweet

Sometimes you'll want to speed up your game, either because you have more than four players with you, waiting over there on the sidelines, itching to play in, or maybe simply because your time is limited, but you still want to play full 11-point games. An easy solution is to switch to rally scoring. This method of scoring ignores the usual pickleball rule that allows players to earn a point only when serving; instead, in rally scoring a point is awarded for every rally winner.

Are there tricks to help you remember the order of the numbers in the score?

Try the mantra "Us. Them. Me."

Point to yourself, then across the net, then back to yourself while saying the score aloud.

Enlist the help of your partner, if they're willing—but it's not their responsibility to announce the score, and they would probably rather concentrate on the upcoming point.

Think again if you think it's not important to call out the score before you serve. If you care about rules and regs, know that calling the score is a USAPA rule, so not announcing can result in a fault (yup, the loss of a point). If you don't care about rules, because, gee, it's just a game, it's also simply poor etiquette. It can be very annoying to every player in your group, not just your partner. When you're ready to serve and you call out some old score from seven minutes ago, it causes confusion at a crucial moment, because others want to stop and correct you. Now everyone has lost the thread of the game, is not ready to return the ball, they're wondering whether they should correct you now or later, and you've got four people whose concentration is completely blown while you've just launched the ball into the air.

Learn to say the score: Your score. Their score. Whether you are the first or second server. It *will* get easier. If you don't make the effort, this much is certain: other players will probably complain behind your back. You don't want that.

DIY Pickleball Court

Setting up your own pickleball court, or one in your community, is nearly as easy and inexpensive as picking up the sport itself. There's a little Tom Sawyer quality to it: it's the sort of job that's easier to do with two or three pals, and, actually, when you promise them it'll be fun, you won't be lying. Bring snacks, naturally.

First, ferret out your location. If you have a driveway wide enough for a two-car garage, or live on a cul-de-sac or quiet street, the hardest step is done! An empty or deserted parking lot will also do the trick. Same with a no-longer-used handball court in the neighborhood. Even if there's an occasional crack in the surface, you can decide on your own forgiving rules: The Grass-Coming-Through-the-Concrete Rule. The There's-a-Car-Coming-Up-the-Street-Serve-Do-Over Exception. The right spot for you is out there—you just need to be a pickleball detective.

PRO TIP

If you have a choice, build a court facing north and south; this way the sunrise and sunset will be over your shoulder, instead of in your eyes. You have to figure out what fights to pick in pickleball, and complaining about a beautiful sunset blinding you shouldn't be one of them.

The Live Area

Of course, you're going to set up your court wherever you're lucky enough to find a spot. But your first consideration is to have enough space for the court itself; for safety's sake and ease of movement, the recommended area is 30 feet wide by 60 feet long, to give everyone plenty of room to swing, run, and act the hero. If you have the room for wheelchair pickleball, 44 feet wide by 74 feet long would be perfect. (Remember, wheelchair players are allowed to—and will!—hit a ball whose second bounce is outside the court boundaries.)

Oh, and if you're up for it? A 9- to 10-foot fence surrounding your court is also helpful.

The Court

A pickleball court's dimensions are much smaller than a tennis court's—the entire playing area is just 20 feet wide by 44 feet long—but are the same size as a doubles badminton court. And here's a cool and convenient factoid: a lot of city streets are exactly 20 feet wide! This has the added bonus of your never having to worry about an out call on the sidelines of the court. When the ball hits the curb or plops on the grass, it's OUT! No questions asked.

You'll find printable dimensions on the USA Pickleball Association website (usapickleball.org). Asphalt or concrete is likely the surface if you're playing outdoors. If you're indoors, at a community building or sports center, a court will often be on a hardwood floor—taping the pickleball court lines on part

Court

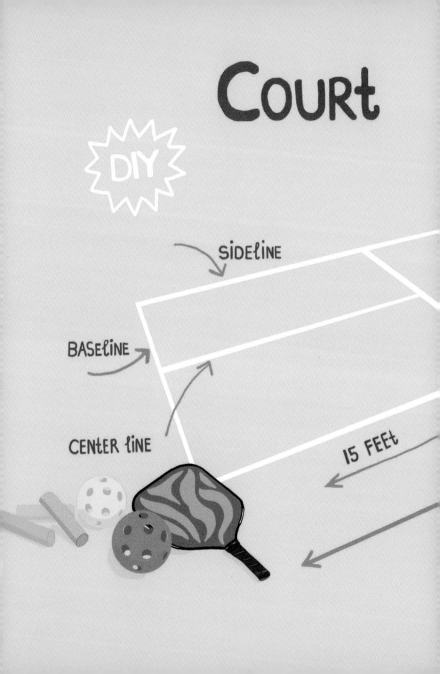

DIY

SIDELINE

BASELINE

CENTER LINE

15 FEET

Dimensions

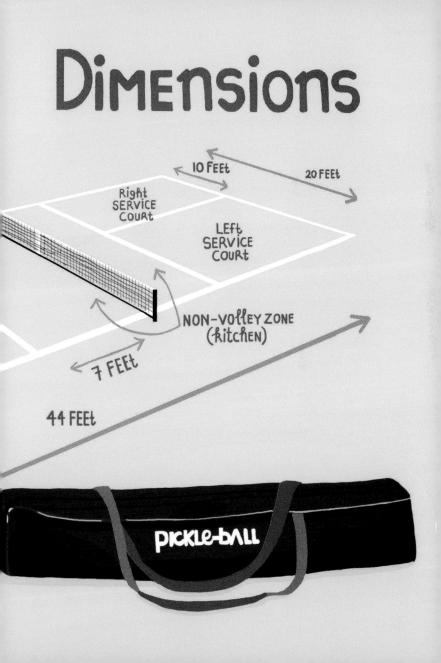

10 Feet

20 Feet

Right SERVICE COURT

Left SERVICE COURT

NON-VOLLEY ZONE (Kitchen)

7 FEEt

44 FEEt

PICKLE-BALL

of a basketball court is not uncommon. Additional space on the sides and back ends of the court is desirable. If you're not lucky enough to have fencing surrounding your new court, you'll get in a lot more steps chasing the ball!

The Net

There is a plethora of nets available, and the same ones can be used indoors and out. Try your local sporting goods store or look online for variety and price point. If you're planning on packing up your net after every use, make sure it comes with a carry bag, and read reviews to make sure users think the net you're considering is easy to assemble. It should take one or two people less than five minutes to put a net together. If you know you'll constantly be taking public transportation to your location, you may want to consider its weight as well. When the net is set up it should be 36 inches tall on the sides, and 34 inches in the middle. If you're going to leave your net out through all kinds of weather and seasons, make sure it's sturdy. Beware of net packages that include inexpensive paddles; you don't want to play with cheap wooden paddles—spend your money on the net, period.

The How-To

This is one DIY project that won't break the bank. A bit of paint, a brush or two, a few rolls of tape, some string, a little chalk. Add a couple of buddies and a sunny morning and you'll be all set.

Outdoors

Painter's tape is easy to use to set your court boundaries: it sticks well to the surface, yet is very easy to remove. You'll need exactly 396 feet, but make sure you have a little extra for overlapping end pieces when laying it down and some to box out a mark in the middle of the court where the net should be placed.

Let's build your court step-by-step.

- To paint even court lines, you will stick down two parallel lines of tape, one inside the other, with exactly 2 inches separating them. (The in-between space will be painted to create the lines.) Your court will be 20 feet wide and 44 feet long. The kitchen area is a total of 14 feet long, extending 7 feet on each side of the net. This leaves 15 feet for each backcourt, each bisected.

- First lay down what will be the outer lines of tape for the sidelines. The measurement between the sidelines of the court should be exactly 20 feet, measured across the court from outside edge to outside edge of the lines. That's your court width. The sidelines—that is, the length of the court—are 44 feet long.

- Next, put down a line of tape parallel to the first, set 2 inches into the court. Once the space between the tape lines is painted, the court should measure 19 feet 8 inches from the inside edge of one sideline across the court to the inside edge of the other sideline. Measuring from the outer edges of the painted sidelines should yield exactly 20 feet.

- Now lay down your two sets of tape for the baseline on each end. Remember that the distance between the far edges of your painted lines should measure 44 feet total, so lay your interior lines of tape 2 inches in.

- The kitchen line goes from sideline to sideline on each half of the court. Make a guide mark for yourself in the middle, exactly 22 feet from each baseline, and measure 7 feet each way toward the baseline. (The far edge of your kitchen line should be 7 feet from the middle of the court, with the near edge 2 inches closer to the net.)

- Mark the exact center of the length of the court with a bit of paint on each sideline so you can put your net down perfectly each time you set it up.

- The only lines left to tape now are your center court lines for each side. Mark the exact middle from the outside edges of your sideline, and your taped line should extend an inch to each side. The center lines go from the baseline to the kitchen line, so that the backcourt is bisected. The kitchen is not bisected.

- The best way to make your lines straight:

  - Measure carefully and frequently along each line you're preparing.

  - Use chalk as a guideline before you set down your tape.

  - Make a plumb line end to end with string or twine and it'll be straight as an arrow.

- Now paint! A small brush or a 2- or 3-inch roller gets the job done fast and easily. Paint in between all your parallel pieces of tape. Again, each painted line should be 2 inches wide.

The paint needs to be chosen wisely. Make sure it has no sand in it; that kind of paint can lead to tripping and falling. It needs to be durable in all kinds of weather and over time. A good suggestion is traffic-marking paint: the bright white, neon yellow, or blue paint used on streets and parking lots to mark crosswalks and spaces. A couple of quarts will be enough. A good, bright latex outdoor paint will only need one coat, and will dry in a few hours.

Be sure to read these steps again once you have the tape in your hand. Then once more. You know what they say about wallpaper: measure twice, cut once. Same goes here.

Indoors

Vinyl tape is available to use on indoor courts. Available at hardware stores, it sticks well on wood, concrete, and tile, and will not trip players. It is meant to last a long while (though it will start to fray and come up in places over time), so isn't as easy to pull up as painter's tape. The tape is 2 inches wide, the same width as a court line.

Chalk is another simple—though perhaps less exact—tool for marking your court. Purchase a big box of sidewalk chalk, leave it in your car with your portable net and a tape measure, and you're ready for a pickup game just about anywhere. A chalk court is quick to lay out, and isn't permanent. These factors make chalking the perfect choice for many spots, especially those in public places, where recreational space is shared or is only available for temporary use. When playing on a chalk court, you might consider being more forgiving than usual about calling a ball out given that drawn chalk lines will be less exact than lines on a permanent court—and there's nothing wrong with relaxing a bit.

The great thing about chalking a court? It sort of makes you like the neighborhood pickleball Zorro: a bandit who swoops in,

puts down a court-for-a-minute and a net, and disappears once darkness falls.

THE Quirky Rules

Lots of pickleball rules will feel familiar to those who have played other racket sports. But you'll also see that you're entering a Bizarro World where this sport's rules and regulations are concerned.

By no means does this chapter cover all the rules of the game; it does, however, highlight some of the oddest regulations, which may save you some grief later. Learn and enjoy. Possibly also laugh.

Around-the-Post Shot

One of the odder rules is the allowable around-the-post shot, or simply ATP. Let's say a wicked crosscourt shot has sent you way offside, outside the court area, yet you still manage somehow to reach your opponent's shot. It is completely permissible for you to hit the ball around the side of the post, at any height. In fact, the returning ball can be as low as two inches off the ground— and that sure will make it hard to return. The ball does not need to actually go over the net to be counted as a return shot.

The Bert

See "The Erne Shot."

Cracked Ball

Yes, your sheer strength (or possibly just cold weather) can lead to a broken or cracked pickleball. What happens when it breaks during play—and very possibly causes you to lose a point?

You must play out the point, even if you suspect—either based on a sound or from the ball's suddenly hobbled behavior—that the pickleball is damaged. When the point ends, all players will inspect the ball to assess its condition. If it is fine, continue the game; if it's cracked or broken, all players must decide whether or not the point was affected by the ball's condition. If all agree the ball wreaked havoc on that previous point, it should be played over.

Distracted Play

A player may not yell, stamp their feet, or otherwise try to distract their opponent while said opponent is getting ready to serve. This is a competition pickleball rule, when a referee is on hand—what you decide for your own casual play may differ. An audible "You suck" is certainly rude, if nothing else; some players are also thrown by compliments on their outfits or appearance. Let's put it this way: if you know your opponent's Achilles' heel, and you use it to your advantage, well, maybe it's up to you to decide if you can live with yourself.

If you cause a distraction, your opponents can call a fault on you. And they wouldn't be wrong.

The Double Bounce

This rule is particularly difficult to follow because you have to ignore the temptation to hit some shots that are just so damn juicy. The two-bounce rule means the pickleball must bounce twice before any player can volley—that is, hit it in the air before it bounces. The ball has to bounce on your opponent's side after you serve, and then once more, back on your side. Only then can volleying commence. Stepping in for an overhead smash on the first return is verboten.

The Double Hit

Yes, you may hit the ball twice! Well, wait. You cannot nick the ball, have it drop, then run around it and hit it again (if you could even accomplish such a feat in the first place). But as long as the swing of your paddle is continuous, if the ball hits the paddle more than once, you're okay. And since the ball and paddle are two fairly hard surfaces in motion, this is not at all unusual.

Now, if you're wondering whether it's allowable for you and your partner to both hit the ball, one after the other, before sending it over the net? No. Now you're asking too much.

The Erne Shot

If you've studied the basic rules of pickleball set out by the USA Pickleball Association, you already know that you cannot volley a ball while standing in the kitchen. There *is* a way to volley very near the kitchen, or non-volley zone, but it takes some practice. An Erne (named after an inventive player, Erne Perry) is a legit way to volley a dink—but you still need to stay outside the kitchen. You may plant your feet to the right or left outside the court area near the net and smack the ball in the air, being careful not to let your paddle ever cross the plane of the net. Or you can remain behind the kitchen line near the sideline and volley the ball while you are in the air, jumping— and landing—outside of the sideline. This may require some additional athleticism. It's an extremely satisfying shot . . . if you can perfect it!

And yes, there is also a Bert. It's the same shot, but made by your partner, who jumps in front of you on the court, hits the volley, and lands with both feet outside the sideline. Check out YouTube for good examples of both.

Injury During Play

Regardless of any injury incurred during play, players continue until the conclusion of the point. Implied here, but not stated, is "if humanly possible." So, try not to drop dead before the point is over.

"I've been hit!"

Just like in some other racket sports, if you or your partner is hit by an opponent's ball, it is considered a fault, and you lose the point. This includes clothing or anything on your person. Even if you're hit while standing out of bounds—behind the baseline, for example—as long as that ball's live (that is, still in play) when you're hit, you lose the point.

In related news: You must not reach up and catch a ball in flight because you realize it's going out. Waaaaay out. Couldn't be a worse shot. That ball is still live, folks, and you just touched it. Point to the other team.

The Kitchen Line

No matter how many times you ask: yes, a serve that lands on the kitchen—or non-volley zone—line, which separates the kitchen from the service area, is out. The line is part of the kitchen and is not in bounds. If the ball hits any other line, it is in fair play.

Just in case it needs to be reiterated, because someone argues about this in nearly every match: if a serve lands on the kitchen line, it is OUT.

The Let on the Net

In tennis, a serve that hits the top of the net as it goes over, and then lands in the service court is called a let and prompts a do-over. Not so in pickleball. If a ball clips the net and lands in the correct service area, it is a live ball and remains in play. This leads to some crazy, hard-to-return shots. Adds to the fun, of course—if it's your serve, that is.

Line Calling

The USAPA, the source and arbiter of all pickleball regulations, has a lengthy "Line Call Rules" section in its current rulebook, but interestingly, within those rules is a Code of Ethics about line calling. In social and casual play, where there are no line judges or referees, players are left to their own questionable devices. And that's where the ethics come in.

Here are a few points from the Ethics 101 guidelines.

- Players make in or out calls on their own end of the court. But if they have second thoughts, they may ask their opponents' opinion. If no one has a clear and firm answer, the initial call stays. Of course, the other, extra-polite solution is a do-over: start the point again. You're in no way obligated to do this. But it's awful nice. Just saying.

- A player should not question an opponent's call. This kind of restraint exists in a perfect world, of course.

- Once you ask your opponent to weigh in on an iffy bounce on your side, and they say they had a clear view of what happened, you can't call them on their opinion. This is a lesson you learned when you were seven years old, and the rules haven't changed.

- Now a ball lands on your side. You yell "Out!" right as your partner shouts "In!" Oops. The seed of doubt has been planted—the ball is in.

- After the point is over, a player may override a partner's call, or even an opponent's in call. The catch is that you can only do so if it's to your disadvantage. A true test of moral fortitude.

Musicology

If you're in competitive tournament play, you've got to dump the earbuds and headphones. If you're simply playing with your friends, feel free to pump up the volume. However, this begs the question: If you want to tune your pals out like that, what are you doing playing with them in the first place?

Out of Bounds

How about if the ball hits the post? Oh, sure, you might think because you can make the wacky around-the-post shot that actually *hitting* the post with the ball, and then having it hop over to your opponent's side, would be a legal shot. Nope. Take a look: the posts are positioned outside the confines of the court. A ball that hits them is out of bounds.

Additionally, hitting anything else that's a permanent fixture outside or above the court is the fault of him who hit it. If you're playing indoors and you hit a light, rafter, or stanchion of some sort, for example—your fault. Point goes to your opponent.

Over and Back

This play is a sight to see, no matter what the result.

Let's say you hit a shot with such a serious backspin (or perhaps a strong gale is coming at you) that the ball drops over the net and then comes right back over to your side—without a player on the opposite court hitting the ball. It is allowable for your opponent to either reach over the net—as long as

Now? Is Now Okay?

There is a lot of misunderstanding about when you can and cannot be in the kitchen. You can stand around in it all day long if you want, but why would you? If a ball comes over the net at you, you cannot hit it before it bounces. And you probably can't back out of the kitchen quickly enough to do so. Can you step into the kitchen in anticipation of hitting a ball that you can see is going to land there, then hit it after it bounces? *Mais oui!* But here's an important point that people often argue about: you may *not* step on the kitchen line or into the area of the kitchen after you've returned a shot from just behind that area of the court. Congratulations on staying behind the kitchen line to get that shot—but now you've got to stay there. It is not legal to fall into the non-volley zone just because the ball is no longer in contact with your paddle. That ball is still live, and an invasion of the kitchen would be illegal, so you'd lose the point. But what happens if you slam that ball too hard and it lands outside the opposite baseline? Once it bounces, it's dead, and so you are free to fall into the kitchen in despair.

they don't touch it—or come around it, to return the shot to . . .
well, essentially themself. Or, if you're lucky, you get to stand
and watch the magic of your own shot going over the net and
spinning right back. The point is yours. And damn, can you
believe you didn't get a video of that?

Ticktock

Believe it or not, there is a shot clock. Once the server
announces the score, they have 10 seconds to serve the ball.
(Remember, a serve should not commence until the score is
called by the server.) So, chatter, trash-talking, sudden gusts of
wind, imaginary shoe-tying tasks can still be addressed. Just
get it all out of the way before you announce the score.

There Will Be Blood

Of course there will. This is high-velocity hoo-hah here. You'll fall,
you'll scrape, you'll hit yourself in the shin. Nevertheless, if there's
blood on a player, or on the court, play stops until it's cleaned up.

What's in? What's out?

This one is tricky. The ball has landed outside the line . . . but
the shadow of the ball, and part of the circumference of the
ball, overhangs the line. The ball is OUT. Only where the ball
touches the actual baseline or sideline counts. (In tennis, this
rule is different, because a tennis ball is squishier, and at some
moment during contact with the playing surface it may have
touched the line.)

THE Lingo

Now, people, it's time to talk the talk.

Most folks don't need to be told what a serve is, or a backhand, a slice, or a lob—these terms are part of the common language of racket sports. But pickleball has a weird subset of words and phrases you really want to get in on. "Dink" and "falafel" and "banger"? The language is as unique as the sport itself. Enjoy the following pickleball vocabulary primer.

BANGER—Although pickleball, when played expertly, is a game of strategy with four players generally up at the net, so many people have migrated over from other court sports that it's not uncommon to find yourself in a game against an opponent who may lack finesse but has a hell of an arm. They'll keep you at the back tape, and they'll use every ounce of strength they've got to slam the ball over the net. "Dink" is often a foreign word to this kind of pickler. Welcome to the world of the banger.

DEAD DINK—A perfectly acceptable kitchen-to-kitchen shot with nothing special to give it a better chance of being a winner. This term is often used to describe a ball hit a little high over the net or simply returned to the middle.

DILLBALL—A ball that has bounced once in the court and is still live.

DINK—The great finesse shot in pickleball, it is sent from your non-volley zone to your opponent's, delivered low and straight across, or crosscourt. Either way, the more a player can employ a soft touch so the ball will land close to the net on the other side, the more difficult the ball is to return.

DOUBLE BOUNCE—After you serve, the ball has to bounce once on your opponent's side, and then again on *your* side, before volleying is allowed. It's *extremely* tempting to run up to the net and slam that thing back after your opponent first hits the ball. It sounds so obvious and easy, doesn't it? Just bounce the ball twice. In reality, what a pain in the a** this rule is! Best advice: If you find you're a frequent violator of the double bounce rule, ask your partner to tell you to stay back before each serve. Of course, now you have to remember that, too. But the reminder helps.

FALAFEL—A shot hit with such a lack of power that it doesn't even reach the net. Often also known as a dead paddle.

FLABJACK—No, this isn't a misspelling of your favorite breakfast. It's a ball that must bounce before it can be hit— that is, one of the first two shots of any point.

GOLDEN PICKLE—There's winning, and then there's annihilation. Getting pickled happens when you lose a game without scoring a point, resulting in a score of 11–0. The rare golden pickle occurs when you not only lose the game with nary a point, but the entire game was served by the initial server. Yikes. No need to define "walk of shame" here.

HINDER—Any action, occurrence, or element (natural or manmade) that affects play. For example, a fly in your eye, an errant hot dog thrown by a spectator, or a sudden hailstorm may all be considered really good reasons to replay a point. If no referee is present, be generous with the do-overs. Next time it might be you who needs one.

I-FORMATION—That's right, just like the football term. With this move, the server's partner lines up behind the server, causing momentary confusion for the opponents about who's going where after the serve.

KITCHEN—The 7-foot-deep area on either side of the net, also known as the non-volley zone. It might as well be called the danger zone. A tricky piece of real estate, this.

NASTY NELSON—Hoo boy, this one really stirs the pot. And for those picklers who think you should never aim the pickleball at an opponent? Yeah, this tactic will steam you. The Nasty Nelson (named for controversial top-notch player Timothy Nelson) is a move whereby the server purposely aims at the opponent at the net, instead of into the intended receiver's box. If the opponent gets hit, of course, it's automatically a fault, and the serving team gets the point. This shot is often attempted when the opponent stands very close to the center line. You might think that their positioning is annoying and decide to show them who's boss with this shot.

Nasty, or brilliant, or both? One thing's for sure: it's completely legal.

OPA—Often shouted after the third shot has been hit, signaling that open volleying has begun.

PICKLED—Easily defined, and something you want to avoid at all costs. You're pickled if you lose a game without scoring any points. Ouch.

PICKLER—A formerly normal person who has become addicted to the game of pickleball. Expect to find a changed individual, but a happy one.

SCRUB—You might hear this term used about a player without . . . let's say, to be kind, much talent. Additionally, it's used for someone who's not particularly good but who enters a tournament when they should be out practicing instead. For sure it's a talking-behind-your-back term.

SHADOWING—The action of moving in tandem with your partner—both sideways across the court and up and down, front to back. In the best of all possible worlds, you and your partner are never more than six feet apart. The purpose is to cover, in unison, as much open court space as you can. Yup, pickleball is a sort of dance.

STACKING—If you and your partner each have a side of the court where you're more comfortable playing, you can stay on your preferred sides throughout the game—except, of course, during your serve.

That's not illegal? Always getting to stay on the side where you perform better? Nope. Think about when you do a switch during a point: you're not on the side of the court you began the point on, and that's legal, right? Same here. As long as you and your partner serve from the side of the court where you're slated to serve, the gloves are off.

Stacking is the reason why you might see both members of a doubles team on the serving side at the start of a point, or one player outside of the court entirely near the kitchen line,

getting ready to slide back in after the serve. Players stack whenever they want to move out of their traditional position on the court. Stacking is also used to situate two strong forehands in the middle when a team has both a lefty and a righty, or to hide someone's weak backhand or forehand. Don't be afraid to try stacking; it can help your game enormously.

VOLLEY LLAMA—Is there a more alluring shot? You're standing just behind the kitchen line, and here's that nice, high shot, coming your way. A gimme, really, until you put your foot into the kitchen before the ball bounces, and then slam the hell out of it. How gratifying that felt! Until you realize you just blew it. Again. Like you've done so many times before. You, friend, have garnered a reputation as a volley llama.

63

THE YIPS—If you hear someone say under their breath, "He's got a case of the yips," don't rush to the emergency room. It's a term often used when someone struggles with an action they've performed countless times before. Inexplicably, you suddenly cannot land your serve in the box. Lots of athletes, plus folks like writers, who type all day, or musicians, get the yips. The condition, which often causes wrist spasms, can be the result of anxiety, a neurological response to repeated actions, or both. You might try changing up your grip, or taking a few deep breaths and trying to relax. Chances are it'll pass!

2010

The USAPA forms the International Federation of Pickleball to help spread the glories of pickleball around the globe and begins the campaign to make the game an Olympic sport. To even start the process of being considered by the International Olympic Committee for inclusion in the games, a sport must first be "widely practiced" in at least seventy-five countries around the world.

2016

Pickleball magazine launches as a glossy bimonthly.

Para Pickleball

You don't have to look far to see a player in a wheelchair on a pickleball court. Chairs for sports are constructed for action and have two small wheels for stability in front; two large, canted wheels at the sides; and a fifth, small wheel at the rear.

Adaptive, wheelchair, or para pickleball is played with most of the same rules standing players follow. The biggest difference in the game is that the wheelchair player is always allowed a second bounce before returning a shot—even when the second bounce lands outside the court.

As per the rules for standing players, the wheelchair player's paddle, when serving, must be below the waist; the player may drop the ball onto the court first, or drop the ball onto the paddle to serve.

During a serve, all of a chair's wheels must remain behind the serving line. However, for kitchen shots, the two front wheels of the chair are allowed to touch or cross the line; the canted side wheels are not. If they do, it is considered a fault and the player loses the point. The ball still must bounce in the kitchen first before a player strikes it.

PRO TIP | **Think strategy, not power. In the end, pickleball is a thinking person's game.**

THE Names OF THE Games

When most people talk about pickleball, the type of game being discussed is usually a doubles game with four players. But, as they say on television game shows, "Wait, there's more!" So much more! With a minimum of just one other player in tow, you can pickle to your heart's content. Next we'll highlight some variations of the game.

Singles

Yes, of course, pickleball is played as a singles game—and a damn fast one it can be, too.

In singles play, where a player serves from is dependent on the number of points they have. As always, the left side of the court is the odd side; the right side, the even. So, there you are: if it's your serve and you have an even number of points, serve from the right; if your score is odd, serve from the left.

Since there's only one player on each end of the court, a player serves until they fault, and then the ball goes to their opponent. The rest of the rules, those used in a doubles game, remain the same—play until someone scores 11 points, win by 2 points, and so on.

Skinny Singles

The greatest thing about playing skinny is that it's really half game, half drill. You'll gain some skills but still get in an 11-point game.

There are two popular versions of this game—crosscourt and down the line. Crosscourt is played exactly how its name sounds—diagonally across the pickleball court to the opposite service area. It can be played two ways: with or without rotation. In a crosscourt game without rotating, each player spends the whole game in one service area. It's worth saying again, even though you already know this: the right side of the court is considered the even side, and the left hand, the odd. Thus, the game would be even side serving to opposite even side, or odd to odd—your choice. If you play crosscourt with rotation, any time a player has an even number of points, they serve from the even side, and any time it's an odd number, they serve from the odd side. If you choose this version, you'll get to work on a greater variety of shots to help improve your game.

Down the line is the faster of the two skinny singles variations, and you'll find it can offer a good workout. In this game, you play only in half of your side of the court, directly across the net from your opponent. You've got to keep both your forehand *and* backhand pretty tight to get your shots straight across in this game.

Canadian Doubles, or Triples

Play this game when you end up with three players, either by accident or by design.

Two players team up together on one side of the net, and the third player is alone on the other side. The team of two gets one service turn each, as usual, but the solo player gets two chances to serve, as if they were a team of two players. Here's the trick: the doubles team must continually return the ball to only half of the single player's side of the court, the half where that single player receives in. The very lucky single player, however, can hit the ball anywhere on the double team's side they desire. Scoring and other rules remain the same.

Mortimer (aka Rover)

Have a couple of extra players? This is the perfect game for six, with everyone seeing a lot of action. The game has three players to a side and begins with two players in the usual doubles position; each team's third player, called Mortimer (or the Rover), stands behind the baseline, out of play. After the return of serve, all four original players immediately move up to their side's kitchen line, and both Mortimers move into their position—center court, a foot or so inside the baseline. Lobs, deep shots, down-the-middle, missed shots—they're all great fodder for Mortimer.

And everyone gets to be Mortimer! If you fault and end a point, you and Mortimer switch places. So there's always a new Mortimer on the horizon.

Aside from being a really fun and terrific game, this variation has some valuable drill aspects: Mortimer can warn partners not to wander back into no-man's-land, and players get a consistent workout at the net. Other than Mortimer not being allowed to return a serve, normal pickleball rules apply.

Dingles

If you scout around, you'll find plenty of drills to help improve your game, but this one needs a mention because it's really a terrific drill-cum-game. It features four players and two balls. Confused already? Understandable, but listen up, because it's lots of fun.

All four players stand at their side's kitchen line, the players on one team both holding a ball. At the same time, those with a ball both serve to their crosscourt opponent, and the rally begins. The ball must consistently land in the kitchen, and *always* be hit crosscourt. When one ball is missed, someone on the team that has faulted shouts, "Dingles!" and now anything goes. Now all four players play the point out, hitting the remaining ball anywhere in the court, like a normal pickleball game point. Here's the scoring twist: each Dingles rally consists of two points. The team that wins the crosscourt dink rally earns a point, and the winner of the point with the second ball also scores a point. The game is played to 11 points.

Road Tennis: Pickleball's Distant Cousin

Road tennis has been around since the 1930s and was concocted in Barbados by local people who couldn't afford to play the lawn tennis that was popular on the island. The sport has a professional organization, the Professional Road Tennis Association, and has spread from the island across the Caribbean and into California as well.

If you thought a pickleball court was manageable, a road tennis court, often simply painted on asphalt, is just 10 feet by 20 feet. And hitting the ball over the net isn't a problem—there *is* no net! Across the center of the court lies an 8-inch-high plank that acts as the center-court obstacle.

In addition to the plank—which is actually called a net, go figure—the rest of the equipment is also slightly different from other racket games. The balls are basically tennis balls without any fuzz, and the rackets are round plywood pieces with leather wrapped around a flat grip. If you want to try the game, be prepared to give your back a workout. It looks like Ping-Pong (and acts like Ping-Pong, as well, with a 21-point game), but it's played very low to the ground. You can find a road tennis kit online that includes a net, two rackets, balls, and rolls of tape to lay out your court.

And by the way, trash-talking is encouraged in the world of road tennis!

Never Touch a Live Ball

Half the fun of pickleball is that you are not only a player but a target as well. Your toes are about as tasty a snack to your opponent as a bowl of chips. With dip. But you need to keep hopping, because if a live ball hits your toes, your head, your shorts—any part of your body or any clothing you're wearing—it's a fault and you lose the point. If you're standing behind the service line and a live ball hits you, it's still a fault against you. What's extra tricky: if the server hits an incredible blooper to the wrong side of the court and you, at the net, instinctively put your hand out to catch the errant ball? You lose the point. Learning to dodge and weave is a big part of the game.

Glow-IN-THE-Dark Pickleball

If you primarily play pickleball outdoors, you can—and maybe do—pickle from dawn to dusk. But when the sun goes down, oh yes, the sadness sets in.

But what if . . . what if . . . there was glow-in-the-dark pickleball?

Whether you'd like to hold a special event in your neighborhood or have some nighttime fun at home, there are supplies available all over the internet that can help you set up a court entirely lit with black lights. Here's what you'll need:

- **GLOW-IN-THE-DARK BALLS** are easily found online; leave them out in the sun or under an indoor light for a few hours before you use them for maximum effect.

- **COURT TAPE** is available in lots of neon colors. Use neon gaffer's tape—it'll come right up off the surface when you want to remove it and doesn't leave any residue. You'll need 300 feet of tape for the court—use the ¾-inch width for good visibility. Also, get a roll (they usually come in rolls of 150 feet) of ½-inch tape to use for the things you want to be visible during play: the top of the net, the edges of your paddles, and maybe your shirt or hat.

- **BLACK LIGHTS** are available online. Use search terms such as "glow-in-the-dark pickleball" or "cosmic pickleball." If you don't want to buy lights, try renting them online or from a photography supply store. Long-throw lights, which emit light up to 300 feet, are what you want. You'll need clamps if you intend to attach them to the fence surrounding the court, or light stands, which photographers use. Don't forget outdoor electrical cables. You'll need two lights, placed at either end of the court, on opposite sides of each end.

- **ACCESSORIES** pump up the fun. Wear neon shirts, hats, and shoelaces and glowstick necklaces to help light the night.

The only question left is: When will you ever get any sleep?

Off-Season Training Tips

You're kidding, right? There is no off-season in pickleball.
There're just more layers.

THE
Pickle

verse

THE Players

Pickleballers' personalities are as different as their fingerprints. But it's likely that the way they approach and play the game is pretty similar to the way they face life off the court. The alpha types are going to be competitive in a game; the kind neighbor is going to be the first to remind you that you shouldn't be at the net when your partner is serving. The lawyer may be a stickler about the rules; the art director shows up with team hats. The waitress remembers the order of servers.

Outfitting yourself for play is generally more about attitude, comfort, and varying weather conditions than anything else. And yet, sometimes the way a person presents themselves also offers a valuable hint as to their inner workings—every outfit tells a bit of a story. This guide will help you identify some of your opponents—and possibly get inside their heads a little before you start to play.

The Urban Ninja

These are the same people you don't make eye contact with on the bus. Their laser glare telegraphs, "Don't screw with me." These picklers love to signal their attitude by dressing in black (with maybe just a hint of gray) so that you feel their venom before the first ball is served. But keep your eyes peeled—occasionally you may detect a chink in their armor! If you glimpse a pair of funny socks or a bracelet made at camp by a child, these could be signs that there's a soft spot lurking within.

The Gladhander

This is a true pickleball ambassador. They'll play with anyone, anytime. If you goof, and you're their partner, you'll never feel the heat of frustration coming off them. They laugh, they compliment, they drive an hour to get into a game. They're a good player who is respectful of the talents of others, no matter what their ranking. Basically, they're an angel from above. The Gladhander makes you happy simply to be alive.

Nouveau Scruff

It may seem like this player just rolled out of bed—but in short order you'll find that nonchalance is merely a disguise. Their look telegraphs, "I care more about the game than any label. See how blasé I am! This shirt is from 1998." Studied casual is their thing. Beware—under this seemingly laid-back exterior can lie the heart of a tiger.

All-Season

Likely an ex-scout of some kind, this pickler's motto is Be Prepared. Rain in the forecast? They'll have packed a visor cap to keep drops off of their face, a windbreaker for protection, and towels in the car. Too hot? Count on them bringing sweatbands for head and wrist, microfiber towels for face and grip, a cooler of water by their side. But bitter cold weather is where this pickler shines. You'll find them in layer upon layer of clothing when it's cold: turtleneck, sweatshirt, down vest, and down coat. Gloves under mittens. A variety of hats. All easy to shed once they get on the court and warm up a wee bit. These are the people you want at the top of your call list! They're game, they always show up, and they have the attitude of a champion.

The Diva

These are the folks who always appear at school pickup wearing the best Lululemons and expensive sunglasses, while carrying an oversized designer gym bag. They may or may not have come straight from yoga class. They might show up to the pickleball court with their paddle in a briefcase. Either way, the message is, "Look at me. I have arrived. Did I say look at me? Look at my look, not at my prowess."

The Noobie

Easily recognizable by the
look of wide-eyed rapture,
puppy-dog eagerness,
and spanking clean, nicely
pressed clothes. You maybe
don't want them as your
partner, but you gotta
love them. You *were* them,
remember?

The Pro

As the sport grows, the pro is finally becoming discernible from everyone else. Sponsors provide their equipment and clothing, and the big dogs actually look put together and like, well, professionals. Happily, though, you'll find the pro still has enough of a people-like-us look to make your hope spring eternal. Perhaps, one day, you'll think, this could be me.

Accessories

Before you grab your paddle and balls to head off to the court, take some time to consider some of the other terrific accessories that will enhance your game. Here are some of the usual things you'd mentally count off before you leave the house:

- ☐ Gloves
- ☐ Hat
- ☐ Headband
- ☐ Wristbands
- ☐ Water bottle
- ☐ Snacks

But there's more. Much more. And though all of these items may not be absolutely essential, a few of them might be the very things you need to give your game that extra oomph it needs.

Hats

You may think picking a hat to wear is a simple task, but there are hats, and there are *hats*. And you probably know what you prefer to wear when playing sports—visor, baseball cap, beanie for colder weather, or maybe nothing at all. Perhaps you're a head nudist. However, even you might make an exception in very cold weather, which brings out the layers of coats, gloves, and mittens . . . and sometimes, the infamous yet unheralded double hat. In a bid to keep their ears warm while still shielding their eyes from the sun, many players will wear a baseball cap with a wool ski cap or beanie over it. Not a pretty look, but it . . . sorta works. The better option is probably the trapper hat, which has both a visor and ear flaps and is made of some type

of warm material. If this sounds like an Elmer Fudd hat, that's because it is. This hat is in no way beautiful. But at what price victory?

Protective Eyewear

Pickleball isn't a contact sport (usually), but getting hit by the ball is common, whether intentionally or not. Remember, unlike players of other racket sports, some pickleball players will aim for their opponent, and though it's safe to say no one is aiming for your face, we are but human, and it does happen. Some folks feel better wearing a lightweight, impact-resistant pair of glasses to protect themselves, just in case. A smack in the eye ain't fun.

Gloves

You can don hats and coats and sweatpants for winter play until you can hardly move, but if your playing hand is an ice cube, all will be lost! You gotta be able to move it to groove it.

Fortunately, there are gloves made especially for cold pickle— and you can find them online and in sporting goods stores, or you can even make them yourself out of any kind of fleece material.

Think mitten—with one extra hole at the top, approximately where your index finger is. This hole should be just big enough for a handle to slip through, so you can grip your paddle inside the glove without the encumberment of glove material between

your palm and the paddle. Simple genius, right?

Carryall Bag

If you think this bag sounds extraneous, you might want to think again. Aside from the usual water bottle, snacks, and towel sort of stuff you carry, in pickleball, there's always the which-ball question. Different colors, different composition, different behavior in different weather. (The ball, not you. Well, maybe you.) So, it's always a good idea to carry a variety of balls for the inevitable pre-match discussion. A cross-body or sling bag lets you bring them all along. Plus all that other stuff.

Ball Band

If you're wearing a no-pockets outfit, slide one of these stretchy compression bands over your pants or skirt at your waist, and you can slip extra balls underneath it until you're ready to use them.

2016

USAPA creates a Juniors Program for players eighteen and under, concentrating on community involvement, tournaments, and general growth of the sport for "the future of pickleball."

2017

The Pickleball Hall of Fame is founded, with six inductees.

2018

The Professional Pickleball Association, the premier provider of tournaments for both amateur and professional pickleball players of all ages, is formed.

Ball Retriever

This inexpensive treasure is a ball-sized suction cup that fits snugly on the end of your paddle. Pop it over the pickleball, and it picks the ball up in a jiffy. It's the simplest tool in the world, and especially useful if you have a bad back, or vertigo, or maybe you just hate bending over to pick up the ball a few hundred times a match. Voilà!

Pickup Tube

Yeah, but what if you've got lots of balls to pick up? Like, if you're out on the court practicing your serve? Long pickup tubes will help you collect all your stray pickleballs without bending over. Then they're ready to empty into a basket. Some versions hold as many as thirty balls.

Eye Coach

Sounds like a misnomer, right? A personal coach for your vision? This is actually a stationary training machine for hand-eye coordination. The pickleball attaches to a flexible arm, which allows you to hit the ball repeatedly and practice those weak spots in your game. Users say it considerably improves their ability to really watch the ball and hit the sweet spot of the paddle with greater regularity. The original version was designed by Billie Jean King for tennis players.

Vaptr Court Dryer

You don't need one of these miraculous machines if you live in Arizona and your weather is cooperative all the damn time. But if you're looking out the window every ten minutes and checking three weather apps to see if it'll rain during your match later on, this is your dream machine. Think of a vacuum cleaner for water—that's basically what this device is, and in the space of a few minutes, it can make a soaking-wet court dry. Sure, it costs thousands of dollars, but what is a GoFundMe campaign for, anyway?

Bandannarama

There will be hot days, no matter where you live. One of the greatest ways to keep your body cool is to put a couple of wet bandannas in your freezer, and tie one around your neck when the temperature rises. You can stash them in a small cooler you bring to the game— along with a lot of water.

Pull Rug

This hack for drying the court is ingenious, and almost seems too easy to actually work well. But oh, it does. The pull rug is a homemade contraption fashioned out of a 4-foot piece of wood, some rope, and a pile rug remnant, about 4 feet by 6 feet. Once you've built the pull rug, picture yourself as an ox plowing. Yup, you pull it just like that. It does a smooth, even job of sopping up wet courts like nobody's business. Even odder, it drips dry like a dream. Attach a sturdy hook to your court's fence and just hang the pull rug when you're finished using it; gravity will do the rest. Are there professional versions of the pull rug? Of course there are. But a hack is so much more fun and less bougie.

Paddle Dog Toy

Off you run to play pickleball, and in many cases you've got to leave your best friend at home. You couldn't get a little something for the dog? Is it *all* about you? Now there's a paddle just for your pup—a dog toy pickleball paddle. When we say everyone can play, we mean it.

PRO TIP

Paddle up! Always be at the ready for an approaching shot instead of being caught unawares holding your paddle at your side when that quick return comes at you.

THE Après-Pickle Life

It's a given that the saddest moment of the day is when your match is over, so it only makes sense to think about how to extend the fun, or drown your sorrows, whichever the case may be. Eating, drinking, and socializing are part and parcel of pickleball life. The easygoing attitude of the players and feeling of inclusiveness invite all kinds of post-game possibilities. Whether a bunch of players bring coolers, treats, and snacks, or someone plans a full-blown post-match BBQ, it seems like everyone wants to make the party last a little bit longer. From BYO to meeting at a neighborhood bar to a round robin of hosting at players' homes, it's always a blast to keep the good times rolling. And it's such a good opportunity to recap your best shots of the day.

If you're staying on site, sideline snacks should be determined by the weather. If it's warm outside, chips, pretzels, cookies, and such can survive in the heat, and drinks can be kept in a cooler. Colder temperatures allow for cheese and crackers or various dips. But a special sport also calls for some special treats. Check out the recipes on the following pages for some ideas of what to serve at your next après-pickle event.

THE Cornichon Martini

A pickly twist on a dirty martini: prepare your gin or vodka martini to your usual specifications, but make it dirty by grabbing a jar of cornichons, adding some of the juice, and garnishing with a couple of the tiny pickles.

> 2½ ounces gin or vodka
> ½ ounce dry vermouth
> ½ ounce cornichon brine
> 2 cornichons

Add the gin or vodka, vermouth, and cornichon brine to a mixing glass filled with ice and stir. Strain into a chilled cocktail glass. Garnish with a skewer of cornichons.

Don't Ask, Don't Tell

Always keep your eye on your opponents. Occasionally, the server's partner will forget to stay back at the baseline and will be positioned up at the kitchen line to prepare for your return. As their mortal enemy, it's perfectly reasonable for you to keep your piehole shut and not alert them. Then enjoy hitting a smack-in-the-belly-button return. No hard feelings. All's fair in pickleball.

Cornichon Martini

2½ oz gin or vodka
½ oz Dry Vermouth
½ oz Cornichon Brine
2 Cornichons

THE Pickleback

The pickleback is a bit more down and dirty than the sophisticated martini, but this popular drink will do the job just the same—and probably a whole lot quicker. If you've never heard of it, a pickleback has a couple of variations: either a shot of whiskey chased by a shot of pickle juice, or a shot of whiskey followed by a bite of an actual pickle. Either is a perfect capper to a tough day on the court.

If you're wondering where such an odd-sounding combo came from, anecdotal history cites its genesis to Brooklyn's Bushwick Country Club in 2006. Evidently, someone came in and ordered a shot of Old Crow whiskey with some pickle juice on the side, convinced the bartender to join her in a few rounds, and a star was born. Eventually, the novel drink gained popularity, though the . . . less elegant booze was often replaced with Jameson whiskey, and a "pickle juice back," as bar lingo goes. Thus, pickleback entered the lexicon.

> 1½ ounces whiskey of your choice
>   (Irish whiskey preferable)
> 1½ ounces pickle juice

Into one shot glass, pour the whiskey. Into another, pour the pickle juice. Take a drink of the whiskey, immediately followed by a blast of pickle juice. If you prefer to bite into a dill pickle instead of drinking the juice, *salud*!

Dill Pickle Dip

This delicious dip is perfect with chips, crackers, or crudités and makes plenty for a hungry foursome of picklers.

One 8-ounce package cream cheese
8 ounces sour cream
¼ cup dill pickle juice
1 cup dill pickles, chopped

Combine all the ingredients in a medium bowl. Serve immediately or refrigerate for up to four hours.

Peanut Butter AND Pickle Sandwich Bites

And they say pickles aren't elegant. These tasty sandwiches have been around since the Great Depression and have garnered their own culinary niche over time.

For your PB&P, any white bread will do, along with your choice of bread-and-butter or dill pickles, sliced lengthwise or into coins. Toast the bread if you like, slather each slice with peanut butter, and lay on the pickles. For extra crunch and saltiness, add potato chips. Cut into triangles and bon appétit!

Easy Refrigerator Pickles

This is as crisp, cool, and delicious a snack as you're ever going to find on a hot summer afternoon—perfect for a post-match treat.

It's quick to assemble, and you're likely to have most of the ingredients for the process in your pantry, other than the cucumbers (yes, that's where pickles come from).

1½ cups distilled white vinegar
¾ cup sugar
¾ teaspoon salt
2 cups thinly sliced onions
4 cloves garlic, thinly sliced
½ teaspoon mustard seed
½ teaspoon celery seed
½ teaspoon ground black pepper
¼ teaspoon crushed red pepper
16 dill sprigs (optional)
2 pounds cucumbers, sliced into spears

Make the brine: In a saucepan, combine all the ingredients except the cucumber and bring to a boil, stirring until the sugar is completely dissolved.

Fill mason jars with as many cucumber spears as possible, and then pour in enough liquid to fill the jars. Screw the lids on tightly and refrigerate the jars at least overnight—a few days will improve the flavor even more! The pickles will last for about 2 weeks.

Cream Cheese Pickles

You can hardly go more retro than cream cheese pickles; they have been a part of the culinary wayback machine for so long that this recipe calls for luncheon meat. But these pickles are a treat with staying power, and tasty always wins.

> 8 slices of your choice of luncheon meat
> (ham, salami, bologna, etc.)
> 8 ounces cream cheese, softened
> 2 teaspoons prepared horseradish (optional)
> 8 dill pickle spears

Lay out the meat slices and pat dry with paper towels. Slather each slice with cream cheese—and horseradish, if desired. Place one pickle spear at one end of a cream-cheese-covered meat slice and roll the meat up around the pickle. Refrigerate for 30 minutes, then cut the rolls into 1-inch portions. Serve with toothpicks.

Pickle Juice

Pickle juice isn't just for cocktails, it seems. Many people swear it has medicinal magic, and research is showing there's some truth to the tale. Occasionally, après-pickle may include some aches and pains, not just drinks and snacks. If you experience leg cramps after exercising or during the night, drinking 2 to 3 ounces of pickle juice can relieve the discomfort within a minute or two. Bottoms up!

10 Important Things I'd Rather Do Than Play Pickleball

1 _____

2 _____

3 _____

4 _____

5 _____

6 _____

7 _____

8 _____

9 _____

10 _____

Are you crazy? There are no better things to do than pickle.

Pickleball Is Life: THE Greats Speak Out

Is there a dark corner of your soul, perhaps just a teeny, weensy spot that occasionally allows you to think, "Maybe pickleball *isn't* life?" That maybe life is a hot car, or a second home, or a better bottle of scotch? Or, heaven forbid, *more money*? That's nonsense, of course, and you need only refer to the wisdom of the ages to be disproven. Many of the greatest minds in history have themselves told us: simply replace the word "life" with the word "pickleball" in the timeless adages that follow, and everything will fall into place. Read on and become a true believer.

> " Pickleball is a lively process of becoming. "
>
> —DOUGLAS MACARTHUR

> " Nothing in pickleball is to be feared, it is only to be understood. Now is the time to understand more, so that we may fear less. "
>
> —MARIE CURIE

> " A man who dares to waste one hour of time has not discovered the value of pickleball. "
>
> —CHARLES DARWIN

"The true secret of happiness lies in taking a genuine interest in all the details of daily pickleball."
—WILLIAM MORRIS

"Open your eyes, look within. Are you satisfied with the pickleball you're living?"
—BOB MARLEY

"Pickleball is a song—sing it. Pickleball is a game—play it. Pickleball is a challenge—meet it. Pickleball is a dream—realize it. Pickleball is a sacrifice—offer it. Pickleball is love—enjoy it."
—SAI BABA

"When I stand before God at the end of my pickleball, I would hope that I would not have a single bit of talent left, and could say, 'I used everything you gave me.'"
—ERMA BOMBECK

"If pickleball were predictable, it would cease to be pickleball, and be without flavor."
—ELEANOR ROOSEVELT

"Pickleball is really simple, but we insist on making it complicated."
—CONFUCIUS

"I have found that if you love pickleball, pickleball will love you back."
—ARTHUR RUBENSTEIN

"There is no wealth but pickleball."
—JOHN RUSKIN

"Pickleball is what we make it, always has been, always will be."
—GRANDMA MOSES

"Pickleball is not a problem to be solved, but a reality to be experienced."
—SØREN KIERKEGAARD

"Give me the luxuries of pickleball and I will willingly do without the necessities."
—FRANK LLOYD WRIGHT

"Where there's pickleball, there's hope."
—MARCUS TULLIUS CICERO

"Pickleball itself is the proper binge."
—JULIA CHILD

"Pickleball shrinks or expands in proportion to one's courage."
—ANAÏS NIN

"Pickleball would be tragic if it weren't funny."

—STEPHEN HAWKING

"You can preach a better sermon with your pickleball than with your lips."

—OLIVER GOLDSMITH

"Execute every act of thy pickleball as if it were thy last."

—MARCUS AURELIUS

"We must learn to let go of the pickleball we had planned, so as to have the pickleball that is waiting for us."

—E. M. FORSTER

"There is no end. There is no beginning. There is only the passion of pickleball."

—FEDERICO FELLINI

"Not pickleball, but good pickleball, is to be chiefly valued."

—SOCRATES

 PRO TIP Watch your tongue! It is always a *paddle*, never a *racket*.

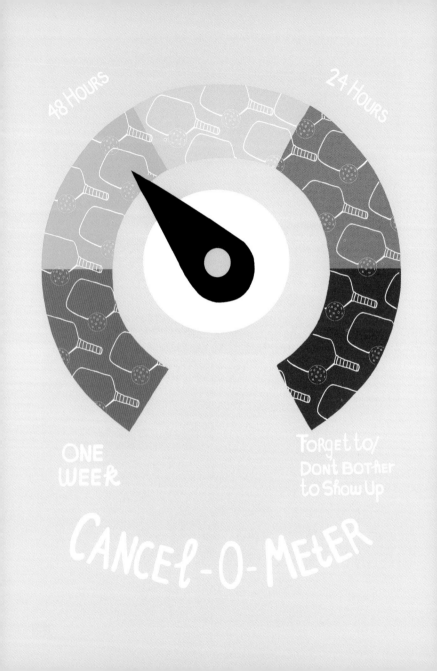

48 HOURS

24 HOURS

ONE
WEEK

Forget to/
Don't Bother
to Show Up

CANCEL-O-METER

THE **Cancel-O-Meter**

Exactly what kind of friend *are* you?

Everyone has to back out of a match now and again—a last-minute job interview, a flimsy arrest warrant, maybe an elopement—but the list of allowable reasons is extremely short. What's not cool is cancelling on short notice. Well, how long is short? you may ask.

ONE WEEK—If you play in a weekly game and you report you need a replacement the week before, you're cool.

48 HOURS—Perfectly kosher, if you notify the foursome host and offer to find a replacement. Some folks appreciate the help; others would prefer to find their own replacement and not end up with your noob brother-in-law.

24 HOURS—You better be really sick or have met someone who wants to take you to Paris for lunch. Same replacement rules as for 48-hours' notice apply.

DAY OF PLAY—Unless you've broken something, same-day notice is nearly inexcusable. If this is a one-time thing, and you're a gem of a human being and player otherwise, you may be forgiven. Once.

FORGET TO/DON'T BOTHER TO SHOW UP—Goodbye, cruel pickle world. You won't be hearing from us again.

NOTE: It has been suggested by some players who have suffered at the hands of cancellers that a cancellation fee be put

into place. Funds raised from it can be used for new balls, for beer, toward a summer home—it's up to you.

FINAL WARNING: It is never acceptable to cancel because you've better-dealed into another foursome. You *will* be found out. Count on it.

Lies TO Tell TO Get Out OF Something AND Play Pickleball Instead

"I have a Broadway audition."

"My tiny house is being delivered."

"I'm in jail."

"I'm renewing my vows."

"My identity has been stolen."

"I have an audience with the pope."

"I can't. I'm vegan."

"I'm stuck in an elevator."

"I have to go to my funeral."

(Truly, this is your last resort.)

109

The Truth About Weather

If you really care about pickleball, like *obsessed* care, then weather is absolutely inconsequential. You can conquer weather! Because in the pickleverse, there is no such thing as too hot, too cold, or too rainy—there is only the correct choice in outfits. Until you accept this rule of thumb with every fiber of your being, you cannot be considered truly consumed by pickleball. Also, if you become known as one who braves the elements, you will always be at the top of everyone's call list.

My Changing World

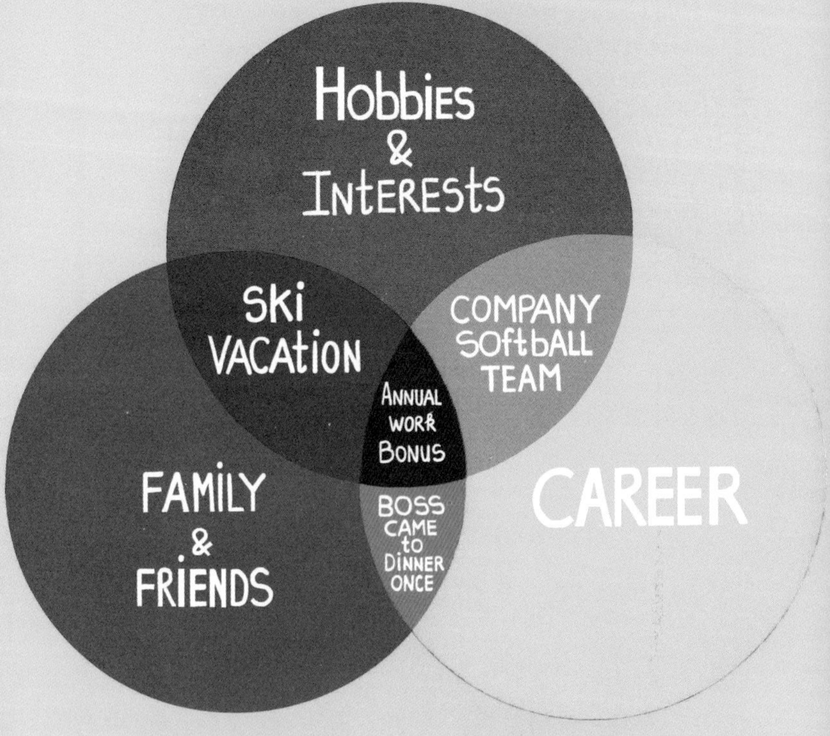

Hobbies & Interests

Ski Vacation

Company Softball Team

Annual Work Bonus

Boss Came to Dinner Once

Family & Friends

CAREER

MY SO-CALLED HAPPY
LIFE BEFORE PICKLEBALL

BROTHER-IN-LAW
WHO PLAYS PiCKLEBALL

CAREER

FAMILY

ARRANGiNG MATCHES

PiCKLEBALL

~~HoBBies~~

&

~~Interests~~

ONLiNE shopping

YOU-TUBE ViDEOS

PiCKLEBALL

FRiENDS

LiViNG MY OBSESSiON

THE **Pickleball Hall** OF **Fame**

Now that you've found a sport you love, naturally you want to know: Who are the greats?

There is a Pickleball Hall of Fame, and the first members of this auspicious club were inducted in 2017. Of course, you'll find among the members the original greats, like Joel Pritchard, Bill Bell, and Barney McCallum, who invented the sport, and Arlen and Steve Paranto, the father-and-son duo who in the 1980s invented the modern paddle that virtually replaced the wooden version of the early days. But there are other pioneers such as Mark Friedenberg, who was the first president of the USAPA in 2005; Jennifer Lucore, a national champion, author, sport ambassador, and popular pickleball blogger; and Sid Williams, who organized and led the U.S. Amateur Pickleball Association (the original name of the governing body) in 1984. Nominations are open annually for new honorees in both the competitor and

Let It Go!

Restrain yourself from hitting balls that are out! If a ball coming at you is shoulder height or higher, it's likely to sail past the baseline. The pros say that about 75 percent of the balls you think might go out will indeed do so. Wouldn't you rather play those odds? Think twice before you swing.

contributor categories, and any person may submit an application for nomination. (Yes, even you.) Awards, jackets, and rings are bestowed at a ceremony each year, and plaques and photos of members are displayed at the Pickleball Hall of Fame and Museum in Austin, Texas.

To read more about the heroes and heroines of the sport who have been inducted into the Pickleball Hall of Fame thus far, go to pickleballhalloffame.com.

Celebrities: Obsessed Like Us

Celebrities are jumping on the pickleball bandwagon in a big way! Ellen DeGeneres offers pickleball merchandise in her online shop, and all profits go to the Ellen Fund, which supports global conservation efforts for endangered species. Entrepreneur Gary Vaynerchuk has become an owner of Major League Pickleball, and inspirational author Brené Brown is part owner of an Austin, Texas, major league team. These three big megaphones, and so many more, are helping to spread the word.

Leonardo DiCaprio	**George & Amal Clooney**	**Jenna Bush Hager**
Kim Kardashian	**Serena Williams**	**Matthew Perry**
Bill Gates	**Brené Brown**	**Giuliana & Bill Rancic**

Larry David

Téa Leoni

Jillian Michaels

Jamie Foxx

Greta Van Susteren

Ellen DeGeneres

Zach Braff

Teddi Mellencamp Arroyave

Owen Wilson

Savannah Guthrie

Nick Foles

Amanda Peet

Melinda Gates

Ellen DeGeneres:
"I'm obsessed."

Savannah Guthrie:
"I like a sport where you could do it barefoot while holding a rosé."

Jamie Foxx:
"Oh, man, pickleball is the thing! It gets live, bro!"

Teddi Mellencamp Arroyave:
"I'm obsessed. It's a good workout, it's fun, you can play it with your kids, you can play it with your spouse."

Brené Brown:
"It's about connection, joy, and play—and the importance of play in a world where exhaustion and workaholism are status symbols."

Serena Williams:
"I love pickleball! This could be a second career for me."

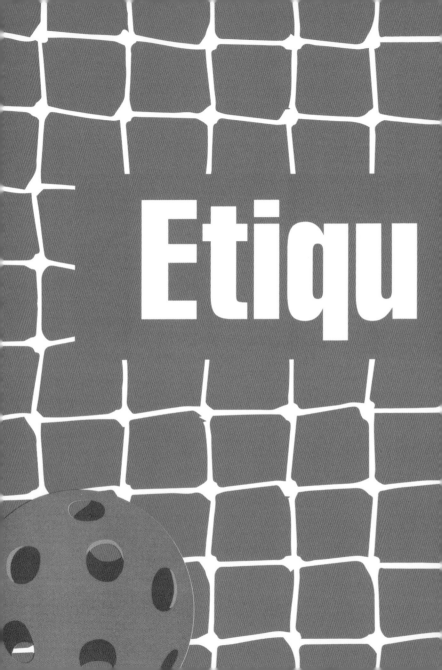

Etiqu

ette

THE Do's AND Don'ts

Do they like me? Will there be a second date? Was I too aggressive? Too quiet? Pickleball dating is no different from high school dating. You want so badly to fit in, to be liked, to be part of the gang. The difference is that the reasons you get asked to play as a grown-up hopefully have some rhyme or reason to them, and aren't just based on hormones. Here are some tips on how to be an irresistible pickleball partner.

Do

MAKE YOURSELF AVAILABLE. Answer texts and phone calls about playing in a speedy, if not instantaneous, manner. You don't want to be the third person to reply to someone who has reached out to five players, trying to find an emergency fourth available to play in only a few hours. Eyes on the prize!

ALWAYS BE READY. Make your car your locker room and keep it stocked with an extra pair of sneakers, a paddle, and some balls in the trunk. You can always cobble together an appropriate outfit. Anything can happen, and you don't want to be caught unawares. It's like making sure your passport is up to date for that last-minute Bermuda getaway.

THANK THE GAME ORGANIZER. Sending a follow-up text about how much you enjoyed yourself to all the players after a match is always good form.

COMPLIMENT THE OTHER PLAYERS. High-five them for their great shots or their new sneakers. Laugh at their jokes. It doesn't really matter what you say: just be nice.

BRING A SNACK TO SHARE. Or even better, a few beers for après-pickle.

HAVE GOOD MANNERS. It's often your good nature that gets you asked back—not just your drop shot.

REMEMBER THE SCORE WHEN IT'S YOUR TURN TO SERVE. This makes a difference. Believe it.

PAY ATTENTION TO THE DEMEANOR OF YOUR FOURSOME. If they're quiet and tend to concentrate between points and avoid chatter, follow suit. If they like to fool around and laugh, yuk it up with them. If they have some friendly house rules, play along.

Don't

CANCEL. And while you're at it, don't be late.

BE A POOR LOSER. Tell yourself it's only a game, although we all know that's ridiculous.

BE A POOR WINNER. Take some pride in your playing, sure—it's natural to feel excited if you've played well. But lording your win over everyone, ad infinitum, gets really old, really fast.

BE A POACHER. Stay in your lane. Don't hog your partner's shots unless you never want to get called again.

COACH. *You* may think of it as coaching, *they* may think of it as know-it-alling. If asked for your considered opinion, give the pointers gently and with grace.

LOB A BALL BEHIND A RESTRICTED PLAYER. You're going to have to figure this one out yourself on a case-by-case basis, but if you're playing against someone who has mobility issues, is recovering from an injury, or is forty-two years older than you are, be considerate. Causing someone who is possibly not as agile as yourself to perform in a way that may feel positively acrobatic to them can cause injuries.

COMPLAIN. Even if the game is not on your favorite court, or if it's a little hot, or if there's a stiff breeze. What could be better than where you are?

Third Shot Drop

When you're serving, shot one is your serve, shot two is the return, and shot three is often what's called the third shot drop. In a perfect world, your ball arcs up and slowly plops down right in the other team's kitchen, close to the net. If done correctly, this play accomplishes a couple of important things: it slows down the game enough for you and your partner to quickly move up to your kitchen line, and it prevents the other team from being able to smash a return at you. If you can't manage to accomplish this move in three shots, keep trying; it'll work just as well as a fifth shot drop.

Salty Language

Rules or etiquette? This issue comes under both umbrellas. Like several other aspects of play in pickleball—line calling or service faults, for example—when a referee is on hand, you'll get fingered in a nanosecond for infractions. The same goes for cursing. Most folks spend their pickling time with friends, or in friendly local competition, where the entire gestalt of play is forgiving and laid-back. Players are pretty good about keeping their language clean—especially those who belong to a tennis club and have experienced being tossed off the court for swearing. Sure, your Tuesday afternoon foursome may be the exception, and at that match the court might be ablaze with a blue streak of four-letter words. Fine! Have fun! But generally, players try to keep a pretty civil tongue in their heads.

Complimenting THE Opposition: Yea OR Nay?

The crux of this question is likely situational: Is this social play or tournament pickleball?

Part of playing competitive sports is keeping an edge, and to do that, you often need to stay stoic. When your opponent dinks a winner, and your internal reaction is "What a shot!" be sure to maintain a sphinxlike demeanor.

But if you're playing in the park with your friends or in a round robin at a club, etiquette calls for good sportsmanship. Pickleball is a friendly pursuit: compliments regularly abound, and sharing them only makes the sport more enjoyable.

There are some who say you should never give your opponent a leg up by saying something nice. Others believe that what you dish out may come back to bite you. Your call!

THE Art OF Trash-Talking

Oh, there is such a fine line between smart-alecky and snide, between a comment that is simply edgy versus one that is barbed.

Trash-talking is personal. And not just personal like "Zing, bro, I *got* you," but personal as in, "I think it's okay to do, but obviously you don't." You need to suss out your opponents if you don't know them well, and figure out whether trash-talking is going to go down, or if it will irk or even offend them. And then figure out when you have to keep your mouth shut.

Words are powerful, and there's a long history of talking smack in sports. You can partake in some good-natured ribbing or really get under an opponent's skin—which, in some instances, is the point. By design, pickleball is more freewheeling and fun-loving than many other sports. Recreational play is extremely social, which sets the stage for a little teasing and perhaps a fresh mouth; it's why pickleball seems to invite friendly trash-talking.

But how far is too far?

Look to the experts, even those in other sports. As far back as the 1940s, baseball legend Dizzy Dean was strutting his stuff. "It ain't braggin' if you can back it up," he crowed. Or there's NFL superstar Terrell Owens, who famously said, "Get your popcorn ready, 'cause I'm gonna put on a show." These kinds of taunts get a laugh from the crowd, but you have to wonder—do they make opponents think twice? If so, they're working!

What kind of trash-talking could lead to you being kicked off the court? Oh, something like heavyweight boxing champ Mike Tyson telling Lennox Lewis, "I want to eat your children." That's not cool. Don't say stuff like that. Yipes.

Hyperbole, puns, knowing an opponent's weak spot—they're all in good fun. Muttering profanities under your breath? Not so much, and that's bad etiquette to boot—outlawed, even, in some places.

Generally, choosing to add trash-talking to your game depends on how well you know the people you're playing with, and whether or not they enjoy some wordplay. If they can take it, some light sarcasm can add to your on-court amusement.

Perhaps a short primer to get your trashy muscle working.

Fake Sympathy on a Bad Shot

" What a pity. "

" That's a shame. "

" That could happen to anyone. Almost. "

" You can open your eyes now. "

Upon Missing a Serve

" Ohhh, what a waste. "

" Next. "

" One down. " (When you manage to get the first server out of the way.)

" Ouch. "

All-Around Sass

" You forgot to turn your paddle on. "

" The trash gets picked up tomorrow. "

" You'd be in good shape if you ran as fast as your mouth. "

" I'm too hot to warm up. "

" My better is better than your better. "

" Oink. " (When a piggy opponent poaches a shot and fails.)

The Reverse Psychology Compliment

Some players will be completely thrown if you say something nice. These lines are best served right before *they* serve,

" You look bangin' in those shorts. "

" Have you lost weight? "

" Clearly, pink is your color! "

" You look like you've been working out! "

And the Distant Cousin, the Jinx

" Really, you've never played better. " (That should put an end to it.)

But can we all agree that when it comes to—well, the Greatest—the trash-talking gold goes to Muhammad Ali. Take a page from his book of bad-ass zingers.

" If you even dream of beating me, you'd better wake up and apologize. "

" I should be a postage stamp, because that's the only way I'll ever get licked. "

Case closed.

Play Up AND Play Down

In the world of sports, everyone wants to play up—that is, with players more advanced than themselves. When you play up, you not only get to see great play in action, you also get to be a part of it. And it's just about the best way to learn and improve. The other side of the coin is making an effort to play with others who are just getting started or aren't as skilled as you are: playing down. You were a noobie once, so you know what it's like to be hungry to play and to want to make new friends and find some terrific partners.

Both playing up and playing down are important parts of the Tao of Pickleball.

In all instances, good manners should prevail. Whether they're friends or strangers, be aware that playing with folks who are better than you is not great for their game, nor is it as enjoyable for them as it will be for you. Ask if they'd be available sometime for even just a game or two. Don't push it—not everybody's going to be agreeable to playing down. Conversely, when playing down yourself, be polite and mention in advance how long you're available to play or offer a future day when you are free.

As for a regular game with either group? Maybe it's just not in the cards. A group playing better than you that wants you to join them will ask, and you'll be thrilled by the invitation. If people below your level continue to ask you to play, but you feel like you've already done your part, well, be gentle. Remember, this door swings both ways.

Target Practice

Generally, getting hit by a pickleball is no big deal. The lightweight missile rarely hurts, though, of course, players should be careful to avoid hitting someone in the neck or head. A hard shot to the throat, mouth, or eye is no joke. But is it okay to aim for your opponent's torso, leg, feet? Ah, a question that's in much contention in the pickling community.

There are those who say that hitting someone with the ball is part of the game, that it's all in good fun—and it's a proven way to

score a point, as it's a fault if a player gets hit by a live ball. Others say that tagging or targeting an opponent should result in a lost point for the person who dealt the blow, and some go so far as to suggest that players who use this tactic should receive a warning or even temporary expulsion from a club. Of course, how you tell an accident from an intention is another question.

A pop in the belly button has long been a part of the game of pickleball, and sometimes your opponent's feet just seem larger than life, and positively magnetic, especially if they're wearing bright sneakers. But in the end, perhaps it all depends on your personal definition of sportsmanship. It's always helpful if you can find people to play with who think the way you do in situations like this, and thus avoid a kerfuffle.

There's No Sorry IN Pickleball

"There's no sorry in pickleball."

This is such a hallmark phrase of pickleball that you might almost say it's a regulation. It's a universal mantra, and, happily, you'll likely hear it from other players on the very first day you play.

A lot of us go through life saying "Sorry!" even if we're not, and even when an apology is not warranted: sorry when you bump into someone, sorry if something happens that is in no way your fault. The snarky phrase "sorry/not sorry" has even snuck its way into our lexicon. Enough, already! Play your toughest. Have the best time you can. Respect your comrades. Do not let the word "sorry" pass your lips. There's nothing, just nothing to be sorry about—pickleball is all-forgiving.

Your

ball

SIGN UP
Elizabeth Smith
Darren Jones
PABLO RODRIGUEZ
John Bridgerton

PICKLEBALL HERE
COME PLAY!

Bringing Pickleball TO YOUR Community: 5 Easy Tips

1. **FIND A LOCATION** for your pickleball court. Securing a spot can often be the hardest part, and may take some work. Scout around: think about unused school tennis courts; an old handball court; empty parking lots of a now-closed mall. You may have to be inventive! But also inquire at your town hall or local recreation department; the folks there might have some ideas about unused spaces, and they may be willing to help.

2. **ATTEND A TOWN OR COMMUNITY MEETING.** Getting your local government on board is an important step. Pickleball courts and nets are inexpensive. Once your community understands the costs—and then, the benefits—your enthusiasm may help carry the plan forward. Come armed with up-to-date data on the growth of the sport and other positive reasons your city or town will see the upside of getting on board.

3. **BUILD ENTHUSIASM.** Gather an interested group of friends and neighbors together. Numbers always help when pleading your case. Organize a carful or two to visit and play at a court in another town or neighborhood. Getting people hooked is easy, once they've played the game.

4. **FIND AN AMBASSADOR.** Probably the most valuable thing you can do is find a partner who knows exactly how to help you, no matter where you live. The USA Pickleball Association has a Pickleball Ambassador program with a ready roster of

people dedicated to help grow the sport. You'll be able to find someone who can guide you through next steps, and they may live closer to you than you think. Find your nearest ambassador at https://usapickleball.org/get-involved/usa-pickleball-ambassadors/. Or consider becoming an ambassador yourself! See more information in the next section.

5. **PSYCH FOLKS UP** once you have a court. Have open play hours every week and recruit a few knowledgeable players to give introductory lessons. We know this for sure: "If you build it, they will come!"

Be a Pickleball Ambassador

Finding pickleball is like falling in love. Actually, finding pickleball *is* falling in love. You want to shout about it from the highest rooftop, tell everyone how wonderful it is, how beautiful, how fun and fascinating. You want everyone to meet pickleball and love it as much as you do. You want to bring it home and introduce it to your mother. The important difference between pickleball and falling in love with an actual person is that with pickleball, you want to share your true love instead of cuddling up at home, just the two of you.

If any of this sounds familiar, maybe you should consider becoming a Pickleball Ambassador.

The USA Pickleball Association offers volunteer jobs as ambassadors for people who want to help promote the growth and enjoyment of pickleball in communities, clubs, and recreational facilities. Various equipment manufacturers often offer discounts to those ambassadors, and some also run their own ambassadorial programs to aid in spreading the word. Here is a partial list of organizations offering programs (more pop up all the time) to investigate:

USA Pickleball (usapickleball.org)

EngagePickleball (engagepickleball.com)

Selkirk Sport (selkirk.com)

Golden Pickleball (goldenpickleball.com)

PickleballCentral (pickleballcentral.com)

Big Dill Pickleball Co. (bigdillpickleballcompany.com)

Landing Creek Pickleball (lcpickleball.com)

YOUR Best Pickleball Life

There are rules and regulations, there's etiquette, and there's advice. If pickleball indeed *is* life, shouldn't there also be some sort of code or stone tablets from Moses? In the meantime, these nuggets of wisdom will hopefully point you in the right direction, toward enjoying that perfect pickleball existence.

To thine own part of the court be true.

How many times are you going to poach that net shot that's halfway into your more-than-ready-and-capable partner's side of the court?

And then slap it handily into the net.

How many times?!

Learn to share.

If you can't stand the heat, stay out of the kitchen.

Ever wonder why the non-volley zone is popularly called the kitchen? Maybe because a shot landing in there looks so very ripe for the picking. You can practically smell the sweet success of your stellar return. But beware the siren call. Stepping in any time after you've volleyed will cost you that point.

Think before you act.

Be a good sport.

Don't just be gracious when you lose—avoid being absolutely insufferable when you win. Who needs a friend who thrives on gloating at your misfortune? You don't get asked back because you're the best; you get asked back because it's simply not as much fun without you.

It's not whether you win or lose, it's why you play the game.

Don't cheat.

Have you called a shot out when it was in? Stepped into the kitchen on a volley and didn't say a word? Cheating will catch up to you. Just when you think you've gotten one over on someone, BAM, they'll one-up you. And they'll do it honestly, too. So annoying.

There are no free rides.

Give it your best call.

Disagree over whether a ball was in or out? Absolutely sure your vision is better than your opponents', seeing as you're thirty-seven years younger than they are? Been here before with this particular opponent? Take a deep breath and concede now and again. Talent will out.

Take the high road.

Take your pickleball with a side of zen.

Ever miss a shot and suddenly realize you haven't taken a breath during the entire point? Think like a yogi! Next time you're warming up, inhale when you draw your paddle back, exhale through the delivery.

Now remember this trick when you do your taxes, talk to your mother-in-law, consider making a career change, or during a few dozen other tense life moments.

Don't forget to breathe.

Aim for the toes.

The belly button will do as well. There's plenty of happy treachery available to the pickler with a slightly sadistic streak *and* a good heart. Feel free to hit opponents where they live— right in the winning shot.

It's all about survival of the cleverest.

Leave it all on the court.

The joy, the tears, the balls you've cracked. The points you'll play over and over in your head during the sleepless night ahead. They're all part of the sweet torture that is pickleball!

Learn from your mistakes.

Play nice.

"Oh, excuse me! I didn't mean to hit you in the head like that. I mean, at least not quite so hard."

What would your mother say? Perhaps, "Straighten up if you want to be asked back to this expensive club."

Good manners count.

You don't gotta be a banger.

You can barrel through your game, just like you can barrel through your life. You may want to hit as hard as you can, put a scare into people, threaten, show them who's boss. But have you any proof that showboating really works—in life *or* in pickleball? Control is the secret weapon of the thinking person.

Use some finesse.

You're not alone out there.

Stay in your own lane and let everyone play to their strengths. There will be plenty of chances for you to be a hero.

Teamwork makes the dream work.

Let!

A word with so many meanings, as these different uses show: "*Let* me help you," or "How long did you *let* this apartment for?" or "Yikes, I need to *let* out these pants." But the worst example of all is the USA Pickleball Association rule change to allow a *let* serve—now, if a service ball clips the net, it remains in play.

But maybe the best use of the word is simply "*Let* it go."

Let life move along.

Stop talking.

Stop talking. Stop talking. Really, stop talking. No talking while you serve, no talking during play, no long chitchat during points.

Useless patter distracts, so save your banter for between games. That's why the distractions, or hindrance, rule exists. Please, let's just play.

Occasionally, put a sock in it.

Hold back.

A common mistake: You serve, and in your excitement, you step in from the baseline too soon. Suddenly, you're a foot or two inside the court, and any worthy opponent will think, "Hello! Let me just smash that return right to the tape."

You may constantly have to remind yourself to stay back after you serve, but you'll be giving yourself some good advice.

Fools rush in.

Be patient.

You've talked so much about pickleball that your friend has decided they'd like to join in, and has asked you to play. Your beloved, completely uncoordinated friend. So you take them out, but their progress is painstakingly slow. Relax: your pal will likely find their own crew to play with, and you'll have done the right thing by giving them some help. After all, you started them on this road to obsession, so it's your job to be a generous mentor.

Remember what beginning feels like.

Be a dink.

Or should we say, *learn* to dink. When we were kids, "dink" meant "nitwit, jerk, nerd, geek," as Merriam-Webster reminds us. Those words probably come pretty close to describing how you think of the opponent who dinks you (according to the current "drop shot" definition) from the other side of the net. Your response? Try to perfect your own sneaky kitchen shots, because dinking is as dinking does.

Work to level life's playing field.

Be more pickleball.

It's been said that even folks who are congenitally grumpy transform completely on the pickleball court. How? It's a pickleball mystery. But wouldn't it be wonderful to add a little more of this breezy, laissez-faire attitude to your everyday life? Everybody wins!

Laughter is the best medicine.

PRO TIP

Communicate! Always call out "yours" or "mine" when a tricky shot approaches. Doing so is the only way to avoid "no one's."

My Pickleball Journey

One of the greatest things about pickleball is that you never feel like you've peaked as a player. You always believe you can reach the next level, improve, and learn new strategies and tricks. And you can! And while you're at it, why not keep track of your playing stats? Chart, plot, and celebrate your progress in the designated areas in this section.

Start Date: My Introduction to Pickleball

Where, when, and with whom did I begin? Best (and worst) memories of my early days.

_____

_____

_____

_____

_____

Lessons

Location	Instructor	Lesson	Concentration

Ranking

Level Achieved	Pro	Location	Date

Tournaments Played

Partner	Location	Date	Outcome

Pickleball Camp and Retreat Wish List

My Favorite Pickling Companions

Name	Email	Phone	Play Level

Acknowledgments

You can play pickleball alone or with a partner, but making a book takes a whole team of folks. Having been in the publishing business my entire career, I know the life of my book depends on so many people I will never even meet, including some of the sales and marketing team at HarperCollins, the printers who get these beautiful color illustrations right, and the thousands of knowledgeable booksellers who actually put my book in a customer's hand and say, "Get this. You'll love it." A thank-you for the kindness of all these strangers.

Closer to home, I want to bow to Team Pickle at HarperCollins and Harvest, led by its brilliant and insightful leader, the great Deb Brody. She took me in sight unseen, and I am grateful and really, really happy about that. Emma Peters kept me on course with the daily machinations of getting things done, and we managed to have fun doing it, too. Tai Blanche held my hand through the artistic development and incredible design of the book, and she also found our very talented, delightful illustrator, Jackie Besteman. If Jackie's color palette doesn't knock your socks off, then I don't even know. And Mumtaz Mustafa made sure we had the most irresistible book cover possible—nearly as irresistible as pickleball itself.

Chris Tomasino is indefatigable and is as devoted a literary agent as she is a friend. Doesn't matter if it's a contract or a case of the jitters: she'll fix it. Like the best kind of friend, she is always there. And a huge tip of the hat to Laura Ross: former client, my one-time editor, longtime friend, equally obsessed publishing nerd, and now, seer. She pointed me in the right direction at the exact moment I needed it.

The story of pickleball's invention is a fun and serendipitous one, and I still cannot believe that the children of the sport's founders, Allison Bell Wood and Frank Pritchard, offered to speak with me. Hearing about the inception of this sport from the kids who were there—and remember it so well!—was a wonderful and extremely kind gift, and it has given the book a warmth and a sweetness that is unique. Allison and Frank, I thank you so very much for sharing your families' adventures.

And, of course, to all the people who got me out there, shoveled snow with me, played with me patiently and watched me improve, brought towels so we could wipe up the puddles, didn't mind when I was injured and had to play with my other hand, and are basically as nutty as I am: you guys are great. We are lucky beyond measure to have found a new way to enjoy life together.